Dichotomy

My Moses Stick

Phillip D. Reisner

Order this book online at www.trafford.com
or email orders@trafford.com

Most Trafford titles are also available at major online book retailers.

Printed in the United States of America.

ISBN: 978-1-4669-9049-4 (sc)
ISBN: 978-1-4669-9048-7 (hc)
ISBN: 978-1-4669-9050-0 (e)

Library of Congress Control Number: 2013907080

Trafford rev. 05/01/2013

 www.trafford.com

North America & international
toll-free: 1 888 232 4444 (USA & Canada)
phone: 250 383 6864 ♦ fax: 812 355 4082

Also by Phillip D. Reisner

Whispering
Time Remnants
Letters to Angela
I See Movies in My Head

A **dichotomy** divides one group, theory or practice into two mutual halves. It is the process of recognizing two extreme positions. It is a contradiction or a paradox. It is an enigma and many times a mystery concerning how to find balance between two extremes.

Preface

My spirit is from heaven. My body is from Earth. I am a living, breathing dichotomy. My mind is a tool for processing and my soul a tool for retaining. All that I experience through brain and body is stored in my soul. After I accomplish life here on Earth, I will take my soul back to Heaven embedded in my true spiritual self. God will judge me by earthly exploits and service through His given attributes and blessings. He will judge me by way of achievements, triumphs processed, hardships, and sufferings conquered. At times, I find myself near turbulent extremes while struggling for center peace. It seems shear existence cuts and separates everything into degrees of two parts. I struggle to live on a precarious line between a million halves, a million dichotomies of existence. I struggle to balance thought and action. I am the glue that holds my real or imagined dichotomies together. I am the awareness that creates, maintains and eventually destroys my unique universe. In the final analysis, I have the opportunity to choose between heaven and hell, but not between the life and death dichotomy.

It seems strange that I truly was before I temporarily am, and that I knew more before learning what I now know. I wish I could remember and relate God's universal knowledge shared with me when part of Him. I came from His spiritual body and I will return to His spiritual body. I am as if only a cell of His body. I say "only" in a humble way, not a diminishing way, for even a cell of God is greater than a complete physical body of a human being.

I possess secrets of life, growth and humanity beyond imagination.

I often mentally whisper to myself: *Oh, if I could recall heaven, recall myself before earthly birth or even partially remember a single cell of spiritual knowledge, I would then know how useful I could be here on Earth.* Instead of knowing, however, I must have faith.

Everything is a dichotomy. There are always two sides, two ends, two extremes and we live on a line between these extremes. This endeavor to operate somewhere between dichotomy poles is called life.

I believe a template circle of dichotomies encompass a multitude of lateral dichotomies in a vertical maze of dichotomies. Life becomes complicated while maneuvering within this maze, this enigma, this paradox of extremes. It is impossible to find a perfect balance or middle flow between two sides of a three-dimensional time/space evolving creation.

Good and evil for example are two ends to one dichotomy that brings us near the heaven and hell dichotomy. People sometimes behave well while other times they behave badly, and usually weighted in degrees either one way or the other. Some of us are nearer to being good while others are nearer to being evil. Churches refer to members as saints, but there are very few true saints, just as there are very few true disciples of the devil.

I seek ways from my own experience by which to maneuver within a myriad of dichotomies. I wish to speak and write about personal middle ground situations of choice, decision and outcome. My dichotomy infested life circle has a beginning and an ending, and evolved with birth and will resolve with death.

So you see I am caught in a dichotomy of here and there, self and re-self, Earth and Heaven. I consist of one part forever from Heaven, and two parts for a short while from Earth. I am an organic entity encasing a spiritual essence that can express God's intentions and further His creation.

I am an enigma to many and an explanation to some. I am a speck of God in a container of flesh. I am a sand grain in a massive desert. I prayerfully ask: *Will I get back to Heaven and will God accept me for what I have been?*

There is a constant tugging between spirit and flesh. The Bible has much to say about this subject. I cannot argue with this predicament for I deal with it every day in one way or another. I, however, cannot deny that the Holy Spirit is at work within my given conscience. God is frequently a pain in the head. I try to practice the fruits of the Holy Spirit: love, joy, peace, patience, goodness, kindness, faithfulness, humility and self-control. He is within every cell of my physical body for He is God and I am spiritually part of Him. How could I not have a conscience for I did mindfully accept Him here on Earth? I did agree to the way back to Heaven. I did agree to live for Him. In addition, in my Christian baptism, the ultimate dichotomy was established, the war between good and evil was accepted, and a personal internal/external spiritual battle began.

I am sure my story is little different from most others. My story falls short of wishful beauty, triumph and faithfulness, but it is what it is and I only want to share some of my encounters that have torn me apart and put me back together. After all, we are all evolving dichotomies because the Universe is yet creating. There is light and darkness, up and down, in and out, good and evil, success and failure. In the final analysis, a body and spirit can only accept balance between hope and fear through faith. Each human being must seek to find a peaceful and spiritual balance between earthly created dichotomies. I believe there are no dichotomies in Heaven.

The contradictory spectacle of life and death is the ultimate dichotomy. It is the ultimate beginning and ending to the mystery of life and the ignorance of death. So comes here now in this book a crude philosophy of life and death through poetic wordage to make you think and separate self from extremes, to find hope from fragile thinking and live life through balanced self-awareness.

I like to think of myself as a mirror, a hunk of glass with a thin layer of reflecting silver on my back. I carry my values on the other side of reality. Gaze with me through my glass and reflect from my silver, your beliefs and attitudes, smiles and frowns, laughter and tears, triumphs and failures. Maybe you can see yourself better by means of me. *Oh God*, I mentally whisper again, *help me help someone today*.

Everyone has a purpose. Everyone needs a way to spread God's word and create disciples like Moses who with a modest stick found power and confidence. For sure, everyone needs a stick in one form or another in order to contribute to society. Life's process and eventual success is a matter of finding one's own Moses stick. It matters not its material or size. It matters not if it is a tiny twig or a huge log. Question is, can it start or sustain a fire?

I feel these days that my stick is writing and sharing my collected perspective words. I whisper pray to be worthy: *Please let me share my limited wisdom in some acceptable way*. I also pray that I don't make a fool of myself.

Contents

Chapter III – Battles   49

Chapter IV – Triumphs   75

Chapter XI – Transitions

227

Introduction

I have spent most of my life learning about myself and figuring out how to maneuver within an environment that at times seemed a bit hostile. I have been in a million predicaments, traveled a thousand paths and stuck my nose in a hundred places where it didn't belong. I have traveled through life for seventy years and have so far come out on the other side with all my fingers and toes. I remain in one piece, with a few scars and mended bones, but nonetheless in one piece.

I humbly ask you to read some of my opinions and conclusions. I was born perplexed and unhappy, crying and fretting, blindly seeking and slowly finding. Things have changed much for I mostly live my life happy and contented, yet fear I will leave this Earth grudgingly and ignorant. Surely, I will find solace in my collected experience, reasoning and wisdom.

I have had conflict within myself many times, trying to find middle ground, compromise and sanity. This has not been easy and I show some wear and tear. I believe that wisdom finds middle ground between reality and fantasy just as stupidity or genius resides at diametrical extremes. I personally cannot live on the edge comfortably.

Of course it is you in any final analysis that creates and lives within own unique universe, and you who must find answers. I only wish to help you find some happiness, sanity and wisdom.

I found this four-inch cockleshell on a Florida beach. It yet had a soft flexible hinge that connected the two halves of the marine bivalve mollusks. I strangely felt empathy for the recently expired creature. The hinge later dried and I accidently broke it, but the two halves yet fit perfectly together.

It seems all mollusks grow their own shell and the mantle lives inside by siphoning water, inhaling and exhaling, and using one foot to maneuver and even jump. I don't know what happened to the symmetrical, one footed, water siphoning mantle, but I suspect it learned the ultimate dichotomy of life, beginning and succumbing while existing in a self-made two shell hinged house.

Chapter I

Beginnings

Coach Rammer gave me this old scuffed basketball in 1957. It now must be at least sixty years old. I was very happy to get it, even though, nearly worn out long ago. I previously had only cheap rubber, outside basketballs. I took it home and shot it nearly every day. I used an out-side goal on sunny days and an inside hayloft goal on rainy days.

I nearly wore through the leather while learning to shoot well. Now it is only a still dichotomy shelf-sitting be-tween fixed historical times and evolving present time. It teases me to hold it now and then, and provokes memories of people, places and situations, experienced dichotomies if you will.

Winter of 1956

I entered my first varsity basketball game on a Friday night at Fayette High School when I was fifteen. I was a sophomore at Pimento High School. Pimento was a small county school just south of Terre Haute, Indiana. We only had about a hundred students, total, in grades nine through twelve. My class was the smallest, but we had three boys that played basketball. My sister Venita's class, two years ahead of mine, furnished one good player and a couple of other average players. My good friend Donnie Bowles was one of those average players and our so called, "defensive specialist" because he couldn't shoot. Donnie made up for lack of shooting ability with aggressiveness and hard work. We had a good team that year and it was nearly impossible to break into varsity playing time, much less a starting position.

I had already played three quarters that night on the B-team and got to dress for the varsity game. I had no idea that I would get to play, for there were a couple of other players ahead of me vying for playing time. There was just so much time to share in the game and the other players thought themselves ready, willing and able to play. I grew pretty tall and big early in life, standing about six feet tall at fifteen. My dad was about six feet four and big. Most thought I would end up bigger than my dad, seeing how most boys grow-up taller than their fathers. Turns out my problem, concerning height was that my mother was about five feet tall. I never got taller than my father, growing to six feet one inch. I started out at the center position, and then went to forward and wound up at guard over the years. That night the coach was still grooming me to be a center.

Phillip Sparks, a senior, was already our center. I think he got into foul trouble or needed some rest, I'm not sure which one, but the coach put me in the game during the last quarter. My couch, Dan Rammer, was once a pitcher in minor league baseball. Some said he could have made it to the big leagues. He was a big bone blond headed man who stood about six feet four. He wore a flattop haircut that made him look tough. I had no doubt that he was tough because he pushed, elbowed and knocked me around for three years, toughening me up for any player that might come along. I used to make him angry when I fought, pushed and elbowed back. His face would get red and he would knock and beat on me harder, but after practice, he frequently said, "good job, Phil," and he never held it against me for standing up for myself.

I guess that was part of my character, standing up for myself, before Dan Rammer came around and remaining that way after Dan Rammer was out of my life. I've been pretty resilient, resolute and independent all my life; it's something my father taught me. Either I could toughen-up or give-up, fight or flee, succeed or fail. Most times, however, I found that there was middle ground. Dan Rammer pushed me to extremes several times and playing basketball tested me several times. Of course, life in general has tested me many times, pushed me to extremes, and yet I've been able to find middle ground.

Fayette was another small county school north of Terre Haute. We played small schools all over Vigo County, never scheduling big city schools in Terre Haute. Occasionally Pimento played one of them in the Indiana State Basketball Tournament. We never got past the sectional I'm afraid because of those dominant big city schools.

I have few regrets in my life and not playing against Gerstmeyer Tech in the sectional of the state tournament when I was a sophomore is one of them. We had been preparing to play them all week. The coach said they put their pants on the same way we did and so we had a chance of playing well against them. We had a good team for a small school and I believed deep down inside that we

4

could beat them, but I was rather ignorant about just how good they were and I think the coach did not tell us the complete truth. He didn't tell us just how long their pants legs were. It wound up not mattering to me personally because I got sick and couldn't play. I think I had the flu or something like that, as I recall. I yet regret that I did not try to play, sick or not, I should have tried. I should have at least sat the bench because not playing in that major game yet pisses me off. I cannot forget it. Sometimes I fear it was some kind of psychological thing and I made myself sick. Oh surely not, I argue, I've had a lot more to fear than something like that during my life. Sometimes I just have to put it out of my mind.

Ok, back to my Fayette High School basketball game. I found myself pushed and banged around some, after all, I was at the varsity level, but Dan Rammer had partially prepared me for such action. It seemed perfectly natural as I pushed and shoved back, getting two fouls during the first two minutes of my varsity career. Coach Rammer told me during a time-out to be a little smarter about reacting to other players, in so many words, he told me to be more subtle and less aggressive, but still defend myself. I learned much during those next few game minutes and got only one more foul.

I found myself in the lane with the basketball near the end of the final game minute. We were up by eight points and had the basketball. The Fayette players got desperate and more aggressive. I found myself in the lane, in front of the rim, surrounded by three players and everything was a blur. I did not know what to do. I could not see anyone to pass to and could not dribble out of trouble, so I did what came natural. I knew the rim was located directly behind me about three feet away, so in a moment of desperation I could only think to turn and shoot. Problem was, I could not turn, could not see the rim and was about to be tied up by a Fayette player. All I thought to do was use my hook shot and put the ball in the basket, but I had no room to arc my arm for the hook shot. In a second or so of time, I jumped high, stretched straight up with my shooting hand and flicked the ball in the basket. I saw the rim at the last moment and scored two more points for Pimento.

I later called it my jump-hook and used it many times during my basketball career, even long after Pimento. For me at that time, I personally invented the jump-hook. It was years later that I saw someone else using the jump-hook. I'm sure other players had invented it and were using it at that time, making it part of their game. For me, however, I invented it at that moment and didn't consider someone else inventing it before me.

I didn't brag about the shot or tell anyone I invented it, but I felt that way. I later invented the step-back set shot. I didn't brag about that either, but some people at least noticed it. Coach Rammer liked both of them. I was probably wrong about inventing the shots. I could have been inventor or copycat, all I knew was that both shots were new to me.

I was beginning to learn that there are extremes to everything. I was learning about dichotomies at an early age and didn't even know it. I was confirming what I already knew, that life is finding middle ground, finding tranquility in a maze of confusion. Life is inventing a new shot when circumstances require taking advantage of the situation and solving problems. A good dichotomy example is extreme ignorance and extreme brilliance. Another example is theory and practice of a complicated situation. I have gone many times from one side to the other side of a puzzle, finding middle ground, finding a new shot, so to speak.

Dan Rammer started grooming me for the center position that Phillip Sparks already occupied, but he also moved me out to the forward position and from then on

I started every game for three years except when having a sprained ankle and that once being sick. I beat out Carl Whitlock, who was a senior, for his starting spot. He got angry and quit the team when I banged into him too hard one day in practice. I guess having a sophomore beating him out for his starting position was just too much. He had to save face. I don't recall his excuse, but he had either to endure or relinquish. He relinquished.

Thus the saga of Dan Rammer beating on me for three years started. Some said Dan Rammer was out of baseball because he was too competitive and aggressive. I indeed saw those traits up close and personal several times. One time we beat Stoughton High School and things got ugly. Dan Rammer said, "Boys, we might have to fight our way out of here, but it's all worth it." He shook my hand so long and hard that night I was afraid to let go of it. I feared his hand might fly out of control and hit me.

Dan Rammer was a pitcher. Rumor was that he once tagged a runner out when playing in a triple A baseball game. He caught a ground ball at the mound, ran the other player down and hammered his head with the ball. The runner was out in two ways. Dan Rammer was then out of minor league baseball. Therefore, he wound up at Pimento High School teaching Social Studies and coaching basketball. He moved on after my senior year. I yet wonder where he is and what he is doing if still alive.

I learned at an early age that some things come easy and some things come hard, and some good things just come without thought or plan. I call this phenomenon "brilliance by accident." It is when an outcome is favorable or when something great happens and you have nothing to do with its advent. It just happens and you look good, you look brilliant without thought or plan. From where does the brilliance come? You might ask. From God through the Holy Spirit, I say. I would rather give the Holy Spirit too much credit rather than not enough, but that is another story.

My father and Dan Rammer helped prepare me for jump hook inventing, but God blessed me with skills enough to be successful. His universe is constantly creating extremes, dichotomies held together with His hand and it is up to us to find middle space. Maybe we are part of the glue that holds everything together.

I have been learning about dichotomies all my life and now I have found my ultimate means of expressing their effect on me. Winning and losing is a dichotomy like playing and not playing in a game situation. Once aware of being in a dichotomy, it is up to each individual to find middle ground in which to operate, to find degrees of success or failure. Awareness of dichotomies is crucial in finding jump hook success.

I have found middle ground in most life experiences. I pray I will never face ultimate extremes of a situation until finally reaching time's inevitable ending to my beginning. I pray I have the correct answers to life and death, good and evil, heaven and hell through my Moses stick of writing. There appears to be a beginning, an existence and an ending to all things, and thank God, I am involved in the whole process.

Into Existence

Someone
incredible in
holy space,
offered
fabric for
my human
fashioning.

Someone
created
earth and
sky matrix as
time beget
evolution in
my space.

I thus
saw and
believed
myself as
clever,
strong and
ingenious.

I finally
realized that
evolution
well grows
progress, but
God plants
everything.

Thinking

Illusion is
mental
notions
executed as
coalesced
awareness.
Nothing
exists without
awareness for
each human
creates own
unique
universe.
One accepts
self and
then claims all
existence by
appreciation.
Each human
God piece
thinks own
universe into
existence and
then provokes
affirmed
creation.

Bottle Purpose

Grapes
fermented
into wine are
victims not
accomplices.
People treated
unfairly
cannot repeal
decision to be
consumed and
forgotten.

Discarded
innocent
empty bottles
cannot be
refilled unless
cleaned and
recycled.
Empty people
cannot be
restored without
reciprocity.

o

Men abuse
vineyards and
caretakers
alike on
today roads
heading
towards
ever evolving

tomorrow that
cannot speak
for itself.

In unfair
dealings,
decisions
fracture,
ferment and
consume.
There are
no recycled
dawns on
Earth or in
Heaven.

o

Empty
people are
like shells,
flowers and
wine bottles,
they are
humbly
altered and
arrogantly
ignored, and
future deprived.

Wondrous faith
floats in
mind and
thought, and
from human
damaged
roots and

pruned vines
comes spiritual
fruit dripping
holy juices.

Cleaning and
recycling
faithfully
makes holy
mouths
speak as
harshness
renders
delicate life
after life
evolution.

Innocence
ferments in
some glorious
quiet place
where
God is an
oenologist and
all containers
purposefully
hold His
Holy Spirit.

Sand Dunes

I attempt sleep
where sand dunes
lay silently
motionless,
not gaining or
losing as
they might on
turbulent days.

Everything seeks
survival.
Even trees know
time passes slowly
here on God's
created dune edge.
Gulf of Mexico is
like an angelic lover
possessing me,
lapping quietly at
my inner dunes,
seeking no change,
having no
evolutionary aim.

How deceiving,
this mighty deep
blue essence is that
teases eyes and
thus mind from
morning until evening.
I must find and
then share spirituality
gained from

water's relentless
teaching.

I seek depth and
find answers within
provoked self.
I meekly hear
water and dunes
quietly share wisdom.
I am alone with that
which guides
thought and grace,
but for now
I will slumber at
dusk in sun's
remnant glow.

Hell's Ghostly Glow

A fake gilded lamp
put into motion
on a long chain swaying
caught our eyes.
You thought it angelic
wind playing tricks,
I suspected devil's angst.
Warm yellow glow
served searching eyes well,
making an unspoken
indulgent tomorrow plan.
An unclean world
conjuring devilish swagger
came from our
primordial stem base.

Jealousy caused
devilish hearts to beat faster,
twisting knife into mind,
heart and soul,
preparing hell's hot
ghostly arrival glow.
Foolish flesh abided as
heated thoughts
cooked own plan.
Burning souls wept as
hammer energized anger.
Rage threatened with
grin and laugh, as we
impishly stepped towards
making angels moan.

Spring Camp Fire

A man's way
is often like a
camp fire or a
burning forest,
serving as an
open gate to
heaven or hell.

Fire provokes,
cloaked with
smoky mist and
glow,
before an
erected wall as
hero or villain.

Fire is usually
controllable,
most times
obedient, but
can serve
ignorantly as
demon or saint.

A prudent man
will let his fire
leniently burn
like a campfire,
effecting not
anxiety, but
tranquility.

Progress

A man lives
like apple pie
making, as
God offers
fruit and
wheat, while
humanity
thinks pie
existence.

Life requires
thoughtful
action from
planting to
growing trees,
sewing to
grinding wheat,
picking to
slicing apples.

A man
thinks and
bakes
all things
into reality, and
finally affirms
life's true
taste by
consumption.

My Racing Mind

With closed eyes
I stretch arms
towards heaven,
imagining an
acceleration
starting line and
racing place.

A ghostly bugle
plays charge as a
tall tree tower
signals a warning.
Aspiration feeds
sweat as heart
seek passion.

Fantasy sees a
straightaway as
body stills.
Imagined brakes
hold progress
until a green
light signals.

Lines pass
before eyes in
colorful zeal.
Mind moves
dramatically at
liberation
speed.

There are now
no brakes or
caution lights,
only star light
encouraging
driven mind
thought.

I don't mean to
be complex,
only share a
little of what
goes on in
my head as
I coerce life.

I simply seek
thinking
dangerously,
philosophizing
recklessly and
succeeding
successfully.

I possess an
amazing brain,
pure spirit and
Formula One
mind that
drives me
too fast.

What Is

I live like a
cold
creek stone as
life washes
over me and
I fear being a
worthless
lost spirit.
I hear trees
above sing
wind songs
while clouds
laugh at
my going
nowhere.
I am woefully
upset with
no mind to
think,
no legs to
run and
no voice to
speak.

I feel cold and
hard, yet
from within
I know
differently.
I am not
useless.
I seek
success as if

having brain,
voice and legs.
Many brothers
serve as
constructive
entities,
on streets, in
foundations and as
lofty buildings.
They give
function and
benefit to
struggling many.

Oh, where will
humanity
take me, or
better yet,
where will
time take me?
I know
there is an
ending to
everything, but
somehow
also know
there is a
beginning to
all things.
I say, seek what
will be and
find joy in
what is.

No Calling

I sit in
lost fashion
while no one
claims my flesh as
silent thought
touches mind
still waiting for
change.

In hall waits a
wishful coat to
wear in a
snowy place, but
doors lock
themselves
keeping me
safely inside.

I faintly hear
someone
speaking
my name as
they provide
brilliant light
to prepare
spiritual food.

How did I
get placed in
this cold place
where light
penetrates
my curtained

inertly waiting
essence?

Help is not
coming for
death beckons
my soul
here in this
demise calling
middle passage
institution.

Oh, sacred mind
in time passing
you surely hide
my warm coat,
brilliant light and
sought freedom as
I wait psychiatric
reconstruction.

Chapter II

Cultivations

Don, Jon and I drove my fifty-seven Chevy to California in 1960. I say we because I had lost my driver's license just before leaving, and Don and Jon did most of the driving. It was pure punishment for me to not drive.

I did some driving while in California, tried to get a driver's license while there, but could not. I compensated for not driving in California when coming back to Indiana. I drove all the way and didn't share the steering wheel with Don or Jon.

Summer of 1960

I traveled to California with two friends in my turquoise and white two-door hardtop fifty-seven Chevy. I think Don, Jon and I had watched Route 66 too much on TV because we got the bug to travel across the country to California on that very highway.

We tried Los Angeles a few days, standing on Hollywood and Vine for a day or so, but did not get discovered, and finally through a friend from home, settled in Long Beach.

We had little money, but planned on getting jobs when finally reaching the coast. We nearly ran out of money before eventually taking jobs to pay for our room, board and entertainment. Jon Thomas did literally run out of money and Don and I had to financially carry him for a couple of weeks.

I got a job at Palley's, an early version of a Wal-Mart type of store. Mr. Palley was really ahead of his time. I lied to get the job, saying that I wanted to stay in California for the rest of my life and that Indiana was history. I did a good job because it was all new and exciting to me and thus I had a lot of energy and enthusiasm. They offered me an Assistant Manager's job right away. In the end I had to lie again and tell them that my parents were begging me to come back home to complete college.

Don got a job repossessing cars and Jon got a job in a restaurant. Don hated his job, I loved my job and Jon didn't care one way or the other. Jon's only disappointment was that he could eat any food free, except German Chocolate cake and for that he had to pay dearly.

Most of the time we had money, jobs and beautiful girls to look at. We acquired and solved problems and learned how to live California style. I discovered many di-

chotomies while California living. One was when we went down to Tijuana to get my car completely rolled,
tucked and pleated with new white and turquoise leather upholstery. In other words a brand new custom interior. Two women sewed on it for eighteen hours straight while two men installed it in my car. It was beautiful when completed. It only cost me about $300, but would have cost about ten times that in LA. Now days it would cost thousands of dollars. I saw firsthand those who have and those who have not. Even though we had little money, we had a lot of money compared to the Mexicans working on my car. In some ways, I bet much has not changed since 1960. I lived in another world for about three months, seeing another part of the country that was completely different than my home state. I was a farm boy who had previously ventured maybe a hundred miles from home, had been to Chicago on 4-H trips and had worked at a bank for a year in Terre Haute, but I was not prepared for California with all its glitz and glitter. We scraped up enough money to get home. I borrowed fifty dollars from Don and Jon so that I had enough money to buy some chrome reversed welded wheels with center spinners. I had to fight the car loving guys away from them, getting too close and drooling on them when I got back home. I was the first in Terre Haute to have such wheels. I was ahead of my time. I possessed a dichotomy in the form of four wheels. I was at the extreme of cool for a little while until others found a way to buy such things of beauty. I was in the middle of a love/hate dichotomy for a little while with those wheels. I understood the dichotomy concept even though I would not learn of the word, "dichotomy," until many years later.

Reverberation

I hear music
playing loudly as
I drive
my fifty-seven
Chevy with
chrome reversed
wheels turning and
spinners flashing,
with car club
plaque bumper
swaying and a
white pinstriped
paint job on
turquoise paint
highlighting
graceful lines.

To ground,
nearly too low,
chrome exhaust
pipes stretch
past bumper.
I occasionally
uncap
collector pipes
sticking out
from behind
front wheels.
They loudly belch
rhythmic exhaust
noise made as
high lift cam
lopes and
solid lifters chatter.

My life is
unfolding with
music, fast cars,
girls and
basketball.
Around and
around
I cruise,
up and
down streets,
waving and
grinning,
showing-off and
changing gears to
reverberating
rock and roll.

Spiritual Mind

Sun through naked trees
can teach anyone to
wish no more for
past experiences or
broken promises.
Captured thoughts
streak through mind,
rewarding truths and
punishing lies like
grained green leaves.
A free mind produces
reconciliation thoughts,
procurement ways and
constructed solutions.
A limitless spirit
surely guides mind
towards a new season.
It cannot be wrong
when enlightened by a
million leafy thoughts.
Anyone with
nothing on shoulders
can always grow
ways to weight
mind, body and
soul with
obligation,
responsibility and
authority.

Hard Times

When cold
hard times
torment and
challenge
sanity,
putting
another
log on an
already
hot burning
fire
will not
increase
understanding.

Black Birds

Anxious black birds
quickly gather,
flying like
organic flowers
on spiritual way
towards heaven.
They grope and
flounder in cool
diminishing light, in
gathering hordes
piercing sunlight.
Coalescing birds
penetrate sky for miles,
wishing to escape
waning light with
breath and wings.
Fall is bent on
passing time by
shortening days.
Black birds know
just enough to
escape winter,
flee death and
find southern peace.

o

I imagine
rain on face,
washing reality with
gentle wisdom
soaking, but
I cannot

cup hands or
coax enlightenment.
I know too much.
My groping
psyche is mantled in
yesterday's season.
Winter is coming.
Hot fire burns
below a once
solid forest log.
Leaves are stripped,
sun is shortening
shadows and
birds are flying
South.
I feel like a
black bird myself,
sky blackening,
fleeing coming cold.
I feel like a
wilted flower
groping for life.
I wish to
black bird fly,
leave organic
drying flowers.
I instead decide
it's safer inside
my mind, in a
prayer place where
rain falls freely and
flowers grow
carefully, and
black birds
fear not change.

Labor

Hands yield to
time's reach as
day sweats and
night waits, for
time passes
hurriedly while
hands grasp for
reward and
eventual demise.

Built caves,
houses and
bridges,
need tool and
labor display
while man's
bold plight
moves closer to
mind over
matter.

Tough earned
daily bread is
soft for
many, but
hard for
others laboring,
building and
reinforcing with
tools and
skills.

Physics

Wheat stalks and
willow branches
wind sway while
soil remains steady.

Flow and fixed are
measuring tools
defining and
providing edges.

Faucets drip,
streams surge and
oceans crash
physically well.

Do you hear
primitive voices
murmur and
warily tease?

Physics teaches
consistency,
regularity and
steadiness.

Liquid to solid and
flowing to fixed
reveals universal
order.

Beats,
breaths and
pressures
measure life.

Listening life
flows as it brings
natural
spiritual expression.

Teaching math,
physics and
philosophy is
sharing life flow.

. Physics is life's
steady enduring
potential and
kinetic wonder.

You are a
wheat stalk or
willow branch
soil clutching.

You are drip,
surge or crash
physically
processing.

You are a
measuring tool
flowing in fixed
authority.

Mooring Lines

Out here
where hemp
tying lines
hold and
keep ships
stilled.

No one
knows needs,
fears and
every day
desires for
liberation.

Who hears
calls of
pitiful ships,
water dead,
wishing
freedom?

Many ships
sit beside
rotten docks,
wishing ropes
will soon
miracle rot.

Fear of
expiring and
sinking
before lines
liberate haunts.

Sweet Ambrosia

I write music
about a place
where dreams,
hopes and truths
get quashed like
apples between
mental wheels.

My melodies and
cords quiver
blues, rock and
jazz that cause a
sweet sauce of
delicious
organic music.

Soulful sounds
delay my fearful
walk towards a
grave stone
hill on which
I shall finally
mystically dance.

Own melody and
rhythm will
lay me down to
rest for a long time
in that place where
gentle musicians
share compassion.

Blind Painting

Doubts
enter a
mind gallery
where wall
paintings put
self first and
artful grace
last.
It's like a
blind man's
cane smearing
blood paint
across a
pilgrim's face.

Opinions
don't
matter for a
blind artist
sees life with a
mind pallet, and
boldly puts
his beliefs
on a physical
canvas with
hand and
mind.

Purposes
motivate an
artist to
see and a
pilgrim to

gain faith.
Both
have a
brush that
tickles and a
canvas that
gives no
excuse for
fairness lack.

Impressions
of a holy
journey
painted with
blood give
most people a
blind artist's
view of
righteousness.
Healing,
however,
appears as
mind sight
changes and
painting
self last and
grace first is a
peaceful
pilgrimage.

Daydreaming

My mind
wanders
further than
sky and
clouds where
no one has a name.

I wish to
remain in
fantasy and
never exhaust
my precious
daydreaming
mind.

I hope
no one steals
my flying
inattention for
mind liberty
inspires
maturity.

Being sound
depends on a
creative mind,
free will to
dream and
find joyful
influences.

Life by Life

A few lives ago
I hammered rock,
saw a different sun,
lit my cave with
wood chips and grass.
I didn't know in a
mind seeking
little that finding
spiritual self was
possible.
Fear camped,
laid beside and
snuggled into
night with me.
I suspected an
inner mind voice
counting and
assembling while
teasing intellect.
Little more than
leaves burned in
my smoldered mind.
I vaguely sensed a
future, but made
only yesterday a
building fire.

A few lives ago
I saw desert fires
in distance
looming while
I grew grain to
feed my body and

found faith to
feed my soul.
I discovered
order within my
puzzled mind and
made reasoning
possible.
Some little voice
bravely spoke,
warned and
winced when
I killed to live.
Weapons were a
freedom use.
I gained power as
manipulating hands
made me strong.
I baptized progress
with blood and
imagined it
worth my while.

A few lives ago
I drove into
deep water.
My automobile
floated awhile,
then black bottom
thudded.
I heard
haunting silence.
I hammered
beneath water,
pounded glass,
saved my life and
made tomorrow

possible.
I prayed
never known
needed words.
My spirit
plunged into
mind and an
inner voice
whispered,
"there is more
to life than
death."

I recollected
lighted caves,
desert fires and
far away life
experiences.
I felt spirituality
baptize body
mind and
soul.
I accepted
heaven's pieces,
bit by bit and
life by life, and
clearly made
God's voice
possible.
I evolved into
more than was
planted.
I became
more than a
grain of wheat.
I became bread.

Respectful Stoop

His back curved with
muscular ripples that
seemed a
humble bow, but
was a false
revealing appearance.
When questioned,
he nodded and
shook his head with
brawn answers,
knowing no other
way to be.
Too bad he became
strong and silent
without choice or
without reason.
His childhood
plight was to be
used like a mule
in time's waking
progress.
No one ever heard
him complain,
this man of burden,
for grace was on
his valid face and
worn hands.
His bent back and
misshaped mind,
respectfully stooped to
some false god of
burdensome labor.

Safe Haven

When rain
comes to a
place
where rain is
seldom,
it makes
news.
When life
is taken in a
place
believed to be
safe,
it makes
news.

I sit on a
campus
bench
wondering
why I am
in such a
civilized
place.
Rape,
murder and
pillage
doesn't
exist
here.

Conjecture
flows from
mind to

heart while
seeking
answers
beyond
environment.
Spirituality
provides
simple
answers to
complex
questions.

So wonder
why rain
comes at
all to any
place and
why life
disappears
many ways for
no apparent
reason.
I question
now on
campus, but
will surely
answer later
in real life.

Chapter III

Battles

How many cups of coffee do you suspect I drank on duty at two o-clock in the morning while electronically spying on East Germans, Polish Shipping and Russian Submarines with my superheterodyne receivers?

This coffee cup reminds me much of my targets, shipmates and experiences while working for the NSA and serving in the NSGA in Bremerhaven, Germany. I understand the base is now closed, but ironically my cup and memories survive. I learned many lessons while in the Navy that have served me well over the past fifty years.

Spring of 1964

I joined the Naval Reserve in 1962 because Uncle Sam was getting interested in my possible help with the Viet Nam War. To be more precise, I joined the Naval Security Group Activity in Terre Haute, Indiana. My friend Chuck Walker, who was a few months older than me and higher up on the list of Uncle Sam's desirables, was already a member of the group. I spent two years learning how to be an electronic spy for the NSA after joining. I was doing poorly in school, with about a 1.85 grade index and decided going on active duty would help me grow-up and find some priorities. Two years of active duty was required with the Naval Reserve within a total of six years reserve obligation.

I went to Communications Technician School for fourteen weeks at Bainbridge, Maryland and was then sent to Germany, the first of three foreign countries in which I chose to serve. By the time I got to Germany, I had my Top Secret security clearance.

Nearly all NSGA sights are on land so that was good for a person who has motion sickness. I knew that 95% of all Naval Security Group activities were on land before I joined the Reserves. Several people asked me why I joined the Navy if I have motion sickness. The answer was always "land based activities."

Time and distance took me far from my family farm, Terre Haute, California and Indiana State University. I was extremely free, even though compelled to behave in strict ways according to certain rules and regulations. The military on the surface seems rigid and disciplined, but in the final analysis it becomes emancipating because there are actually limited spelled out rules. One does not have to guess what to do or how to do it. One only has to do a few things the correct military way. I guess dying would be one of those simple ways of doing things. The military teaches everyone how to live and die, and gives reasons for both. That seemed a lot less complicated than civilian life. I learned discipline and reasons for discipline. I learned how to gain self-control. I learned responsibility and consequences for and lack of it. I learned maturity through time, distance and freedom. I learned how to maneuver within a few military extremes.

I could go into my spying on the East Germans, Poles and Russians, go into how I traveled all over Europe or go into detail about socializing with my fellow sailors and the German people, but I won't here and now. Let me just say that all aspects of living in Europe and the Navy brought me closer to a point of "knowing myself," and finding direction to my life. I began to see the world as black and white, while realizing that I had to live in the gray part of it. I was again learning about dichotomies, but had not yet really learned the definition. I knew the word, but had not lived the word. I realized that there is nearly always compromise within extremes except when principles are involved. I learned that I should have few principles because I might have to go to war over them some day. I am yet a man of few principles. They are well etched in the concrete part of my mind.

I went back to school after the Navy, went back to college, earning a grade point average of 3.8 for the next two years. I then averaged a 3.9 while getting an MS degree. I found simple responsibility, discipline and maturity in a complicated maze of contrasts. I found simplicity and flexibility by following a few rigid rules, and doing much of what the world expected of me. I have no regrets about going into the Navy, serving seven years total in the reserves. I am proud that I gave two years of my life on active duty for my country. It was a small price to pay compared to so many who have paid the ultimate price. I love my country and flag. I got more than I gave.

I Wish

I wish
most world
dichotomies
would be
more like
time between
dawn and
dusk.
I wish
similarity of
noon and
midnight be
understood
rather than
differentiated.
I wish
everyone lived
mentally and
physically in
one peaceful
noon interlude.
Maybe
I should
not wish, but
pray these
middle affairs
be possible.

Finally Home

I lay rotting on
earthen bed,
among patient
wild flowers,
grass and
tree sprouts with
awareness of
true life.
I nearly forget
tall standing,
wind swaying and
leaf producing.

Scary wind
shook heart,
broke spirit and
laid me to rest
after to earth
swiftly falling.

I was called
"junk wood,"
fearing life
useless and
without hope.
Yet in time,
I realized
within my
knurly grain that
I provided
substance,
beauty and
future seeds.

My rotting
discolored
essence is earth
enrichment,
organic matter,
another's
original hope.
My dank odor
earthen bed
knows me,
holds me and
accepts my
precious nature.
I am home.

o

So gaze not
upon me with
sorrow for
I am like a
natural
tree waiting.
I am an aware
life essence,
wishing dignity
when placed
in an earthen
bed of divine
patience.

Gravity Fair

Sweet Lilly's
beauty soaked
my eyes
at this year's
Gravity Fair.
Her splendor
taught and
eye filled me
like a scholar
seeking a
higher degree.

I matured in a
dark room of
misplaced
innocence and
expanded
confidence.
My pleasure
expanded in a
soft lush bed of
down and
roses.

Sweet Lilly
touched
my lust and
made me
groan.
I was like an
injured hooligan
expressing
pain from a

broken window
glass cut while
breaking into
her heart.

Seems there is
little difference
between
expressed
pleasure and
pain.
I nearly
died in
her morning
spirit and
late for
dinner soul.

Gravity Fair is a
wonderful
place to
study physics,
chemistry and
anatomy.
Gravity Fair
learning will
make a young
educated man
even wiser.

Akin to Trees

Heroic trees
must watch
their frightful
destruction.
They are
cut down,
stripped and
hauled away
without
objection.

Cold dirt
accepts
brothers and
sisters
willing to
lay still while
acquiescing
their precious
spirit to
logger desire.

They are
downed like
silent children
crafted into
warriors.
Ironically,
some serve as
coffins for
deceased wood
conspirators.

Wooden coffins
silently help
mourners say
good-bye to
those frightening
loggers,
millers and
consumers of
trees without
objection.

Arboreal Thought

Oh, please with
whom I exist,
accept flight and
give grace for
I have fearlessly
come a long way.

I count events,
express my heart,
mind and soul.
A delicate balance
dances within
my mind like a
wind tossed tree
whispering
foreign sounds,
speaking unknown
languages.

I know an
internal light
delicately sways
like a leaf
paddling wind,
like time
straining with
roots enabling
evolution.
I bend and
conform with
grace and hope,
asking not
blessing of

survival seed.
I only weep for
time's courageous
reward.

No one
suspected
arboreal
evolution or
believed in
winged
possibilities.
And, now
mind is wing and
flight is thought.
Possibilities
mind fly
like small
dinosaurs once
leaped.

Oh, please with
whom I exist,
accept flight and
give grace for
I have fearlessly
come a long way.

Incomplete Shadows

A young man,
down street,
volunteered to
wage war.
Reason rendered
made no sense to
mother, but
father understood.

He came home with
one leg missing and
one eye blind.
Father shook
his hand,
seeing big picture.
Mother could only
fill eyes with
blinding tears.

o

Torment tears
flood hearts
down a street
where another
hero still rests,
laid upon a
community site,
while pastor
claims victory and
many thank
God,
he was not

their own.
Many weep as
long shadows
drift sunlight's
broken silence.

A grateful,
benevolent few
stand close and
later sleep
better for
one damaged,
living shadow
yet lives.
His one eye
watches,
feeling guilty that
another
forever sleeps.

More Respectful

Against
desperate sand
altering waves
collide.
I seek
relief from
endless
assaulting sea.
I join a
endless battle
between
harsh sea and
yielding beach.
Nature remains
constant
through eternal
struggle as
I become more
through brief
learning minutes.

A sea teaches
well with
infinite
power that
shapes and
transforms
men.
It beats body,
mind and
soul with
relentless
energy and

tows brave
men into its
cold bosom.

It tries to
draw me into
its ceaseless
hungry jaws and
wash me
seaward as
I desperately
fight against
its relentless
elements.
I finally
drag my
battered body
onto an
uncommitted
shore,
victorious,
wiser and
more respectful.

Shine Language

Being
complicated
enough to
match
complicated
world
expectations,
is surely to
perceive and
describe
complicated
situations with
magnificent
words and
gestures.

Life is a
meandering
proposition,
heading
towards an
unknown
ending
instigated by
complications,
paid for with
experience and
culminated
with a few
magnificent
shining words.

His Hand

A calloused
hand extends to
greet and
hold for a while.
Humble strength
well shows as
eyes penetrate,
smile erupts and
I cannot
resist his charm.

He gently
touches my face,
roughly pats
my shoulder,
makes me
happy with that
hand, and
lightens my
spirit with
gratitude.

It is a
miracle human
tool of bone,
muscle and skin,
an organic
machine of
biological
beauty, and no
accidental
joining of
spirit and soul.

I know every
line and crease,
every scar and
vein on that
suntanned hand.
I studied
it for fifty
admiring years and
never lost faith
in what it
could accomplish.

Weaker now,
not so athletic,
but when it
reaches for
my hand,
I know true
extended
humility and
sharing love.

Salty Energy

New blue overalls with
shiny metal strap buckles,
draped over shoulders
decorate a six year old boy.
He is like a new shiny ship,
eager to sail and be glory bound.

His eyes shimmer,
large as nickels,
bright sea blue colored.
He gracefully moves with
noticeable innocence.
It is like some compelling,
invisible, salty energy
willingly propels him.

o

Now eighty years later,
he's like an old salty sea
subjected ship with
rotted and torn planks,
lost pegs and rusted nails.
Sailing is impossible for
one who has existed long,
daringly sailed far horizons and
challenged many seas well.
Through dim sea blue eyes,
boyish attitude yet glimmers.
His now dull teeth yet
provide an amiable smile that
gathers to one mouth corner.

o

His created
history is
like an old sea
inscribed log that
lives beyond
sea crashing
energy and
salty
content spirit,
courageously
accrued and
well retained.

He is a child's
blueprint and
design for a
fulfilling life.
He is a humble
heart and
soul example of
boyish dreams
fulfilled,
embedded in a
yet fantasizing,
sea blue mind.

Desperate Drought

Mind in
time feeds
imagination.

Eyes see
day wakening
spirits.

Western sky
clouds at
dusk drift.

Time teases
ominous
rain clouds.

Soil begs
old men to
pray.

Fish slumber
silent creek
water.

Mind stirs
reluctant
ideas.

Rain drops
percolate
Earth.

Big thoughts
worthy
wait.

Little rewards
mend
fears.

Spirits love
eager
fertile land.

Imagination
drinks
vitality.

Intelligence
offsets
drought.

Spirits
feed off
themselves.

Mind's eye
motivates
happiness.

Silent Value

Cherish pending
rain more than
existing lightening,
for lightening is
only an emerging
rain alert.
Some how
greatly value
emerging buds for
rose petals
soon fall with
conspicuous ending.
Nature is for
silent eyes and
ears while
humanity is for
transforming
hands and minds.
Ideas, signs and
impressions are
curious as rain, a
rose representing
silence or a
speechless man
lost in thought.
Civilization
flows beautifully,
giving value and
thus appraisal to
ears listening and
minds speaking.

Testing Ground

I take life
seriously with a
dubious
salt grain.
I fear
beginning and
ending both
will be quite
shocking.
I roam Earth's
middle years,
like a bison
seeking grass,
like a student
seeking insight.
My brief stay
wishes more
pitiless time
with disorder,
whim and prayer.
I cautiously use
senses while
crawling and
walking.
Direction has
no wisdom while
easily pointing and
provides no
friendly answers.
I am in life's
final analysis only a
salt grain on an
uncaring flat.

Chapter IV

Triumphs

My mother gave me this railroadman's pocket watch in 1970, the year my son was born. I never carry it, but take it out of a wooden memento box occasionally to look at it. She gave it to me for no apparent reason, except maybe to remind me that time is short, especially when young and unaware of it.

The pocket watch yet works if I tighten its spring and let it tick. It also works in another way if I just look at it while remembering Louise, and let time tick within me. She yet teaches even after all these years beyond her passing.

Spring of 1970

My son Brook was born in March of 1970 and I measure much of my life time-line from that particular year. It was a beginning of many battles, which made me grow and find myself. I had finished my Naval Reserve obligation, got married, earned my BS and MS degrees and had begun teaching at Tuttle Junior High School. I had purchased and remodeled my first house, bought my first new car and started coaching. The next thing to do was have a couple of children of which Brook was the first and Kristen the second. Everything was moving in the right direction, or so it seemed. The only thing I had instead of the white picket fence was a chain-link fence.

Brook was born after about twenty-four hours of labor. He was reluctant to come out and was later reluctant to do many things, such as walk, talk and cooperate, but that is another story. He turned out great after we coaxed him into listening, learning and cooperating.

Kristen was born in the morning of March 1972. Her mother received a special drug called "buecaldip," that caused her to begin labor much quicker than the first time with Brook. There is an example of a dichotomy: use a drug to speed up labor, but then increased pain requires another drug that slows labor. The doctor administered the drug and said he would be back later, but later was not good because Barbara began dilating immediately. The nurse remarked, when checking to see how things were progressing, that Kristen was coming out and that she had to get Barbara into the delivery room right away. Fathers were not allowed in the delivery room in those days, but I was close to the time of delivery there in the hospital room. Mrs. Lafoe delivered Kristen and Dr. Howland finished the delivery during the last few minutes.

Both of my first two children were miracles, but I did not fully realize the gravity and grace of their births. Oh, I was happy and realized it was a wonderful thing, but I did not fully realize the whole reproduction thing, the humanity thing, the God thing. I had to learn that through time and experience. I did not naturally love them at first, but had to learn to love them. I did not appreciate them enough at first, but learned their preciousness as time passed and they taught me about God's plan.

It is strange how I keep loving and appreciating them more with each passing year, and now here they are forty and forty-two years old. I later had my twins and fully realized the miracle taking place, and now I have grandchildren. I certainly love and appreciate all of them.

I look back at the time Brook was born and realize how much I have grown, matured and learned about myself. Children are wonderful teachers. I probably learned more about life from my own children and other people's children than I ever taught my students. I tried to teach my children and my students to be good people, have respect for others and find honor in their behavior. Most everything seems to work out so that we get more than we give. My life is certainly like that, for I seemingly have given little and received much. I am blessed.

It also scares me a little to think that the universe is a balance of positives and negatives, a balance of dichotomies and eventually everything requires calibration. I fear I have lived on the positive side too much and the negative will catch-up with me. I fear there will be a price to pay some day.

Life Is

I reach
summit at
dusk as
clouds reflect
sun remnants.
In dimness
I begin
journey's
second half,
but now
descending
a dusty
dry path.

Mountain after
mountain,
dawn to dusk
I plod
wrapped in
hope,
grounded in
faith.
I seek
unknown
tomorrow with
tear filled
eyes.

I am
alone
searching
for a place
to freely be.

I walk and
stumble,
seek and
find as
miraculous
mountains
continually
appear.

Seems life
is a dirty
uncertain
journey on a
convoluted
path while
traveling
upward and
downward,
towards a
mysterious
belonging
finale.

Morning Reality

In middle of
night
rose bushes
humbly bowed as
spirits swept air and
sweet scented them.
Green leaves
paved a path for
delicate angel feet
walking towards an
opened door.
In a house,
upstairs and
through a doorway,
heaven's emissaries
moved.
They gazed at a
sleeping creature
through cherub
eyes.
Sacred hands
stroked head with
mindful certainty.
Spiritual world
opened godly
attention, and in
grace of night
rose flower aroma
drenched air.
Angels sang truth with
faithful melodic
words of heavenly
source.

Child like
faith arose within a
dream, as if
little was known and
much to trust was
comprehended.
Another
became one with
original first while
speaking an
ageless language.
Spirituality
bloomed and
flourished like
rose bushes outside
bedroom window.
Sweet aroma
ascended with
accepted creatures in
spiritual arms.
A forever
night dream
became
morning reality.
On unity
God smiled
while angels sang
hallelujah.
Love was
consummated.

My Dirty Face

Can a dirty
face be
washed with a
mother's wish?
Can a broach
worn around
her soft neck
cause mending?

On my
marked face
expressions rest.
I wish them to fall
like grime and
make me attractive.
They surely
assess personal
security and
insecurity.

Someone holds
my fate in hands.
Worn around
neck broach is
not of gold or
jewels, but of
fluted steel.
It's a tool for
accomplishing
wishes and
desires.

Gray sky teases
rain to cleanse
my dirty face, but
it is surely
my eyes that
already hold
enough rain to
purify my soul.
I am surely more
than thought.

Fluted broach
reveals that
own hands help
wash face, but
it is He who
holds face and
blessed broach,
secures fate and
gives birth to
tomorrow.

I fear not
dirty face or
wishing tool
for I am surely
in hands of
another.
I relent and
today seek
tomorrow for
Father
watches over
us all.

My World Is Gone

My struggle
begins and
ends with me.
Questions evade
answers from
birth to death,
wishing seclusion.

Like a lost
war bullet,
I know only
simplicity,
know only
vaulted truth,
dirt buried.

I yet hear
bugle calls and
emancipated
voices singing, and
see war scars
while recalling
freedom battles.

My world is a
mind state,
verified by unique
battling spirits and
pious souls
trying to answer
my questions.

Fulfillment

A wild rose bush
vaguely stands in
chilly woodland
shadows.
Something special is
about to occur,
for a secret
coded natural
message is in
Mother Nature's
genealogy.

She has a way to
life bring and
fruit beget with an
ever loving
process and a
disciplined touch.
As cold rain
alters earth and
washes small
new leaves
clinging to life,
something special is
occurring.

New briers
burst to serve as a
natural defense.
Rose bush
rejoices as
sunlight speaks
buds into

existence, and
through some
unknown ability,
life bursts forth.
Bush spreads
outward as if
reaching for
life beyond
anchoring roots.
It seems to
gaze skyward,
knowing a
higher power
within its realm
chooses life.

Glory stretches
undeniable limits as
Earth expands
determination for
anxious weeks,
then resolve for
blossoming months.
Small pink flowers
burst into being as
aroma fills air with
promising outcomes.

Timely rewards
emerge as if
pink blossoms
hang waiting for
admiration and
then someone's
selective
picking hand as

Mother patiently
waits and
finally puts down
her precious
calendar.

She casually
allows self
consumption as
her natural coded
genetic faith guides
every life planned
progression.
And like a
rose bush,
everything exercises
its natural essence and
coded existence.
Everything
possesses a precious
emerging
knowledge and
thus a natural
sacrificial
fulfilling purpose.
Oh, for sure
something special is
occurring.

Silently Waiting

Maple trees
stand silently,
waiting wind's
loving caress.
I too wait for
loving wind to
share wisdom.

I faintly hear of
glorious tree
given shape and
intricate branch
plans, and leaves
enough for
artful display.

A whispering
foliage voice
speaks of natural
expectations,
but not of my
purpose or
appraising gifts.

It speaks not of
my own shape,
branch and leaf
plans nor how
I can please and
lend wonderful
cooling shade.

Western Mountains

My oldest daughter
traveled to Chicago,
took then a turn
towards Colorado,
came face to
face with destiny,
married him and
now is raising
three kids.
She visits
each summer,
bringing Colorado
joy to Indiana,
yet looks over
her shoulder as
western parts
call for return.
I love her
adoring visits,
love her found
freedom,
adventure and
mysterious
mountains.

My son
traveled to
Florida,
then moved to
Montana,
then traversed to
Memphis.
He yet longs for

mountains and
open spaces.
He seldom
visits, but
I think there's
yet a place in
his heart for
Indiana, but
I think
Montana
calls and
some day
he will go
west again.

I love both
children's
freedom and
discovery of
mysterious
mountains, but
I suspect a
Hoosier influence
home reminds.
We have all
witnessed those
mountains and
oceans also, but
all three of
us remember
being humbly
born of
Indiana dirt and
ash.

Wishing Stones

My daughter's
hand upon mine,

like a flower placed,
causes heart to sing.

We always cast
special stones in

our wishing creek
near my house.

I silently wish
same wish again.

It never changes as
time and life change.

"Near we shall always be,
until adult life draws

her to a far adventure or
my hand can no more

cast wishing stones
near my house."

I silently wish while
tossing another stone.

With Me

I took a
photograph and
caught her motionless.
It was a study of
essence stilled and
grace detailed.
Soft sunlight
through shimmering
tree leaves
highlighted her face.
Her relaxed attitude
momentarily showed
while leaning against a
wooden fence post.
Her expectant eyes
epitomized joy.
I could see peace
on her face.
I knew
she belonged
in that place,
at that time,
with me.

Concerted Way

He favored a
restrained
middle world of
unpretentious
good and
evil dwelling.

Blues music
quivered soul
in a fleeting
place where
remembered
yesterday
walked with
destined
tomorrow
sorrow waiting.

Emphasized
boundaries
contained visual
order like
black notes on
crumpled paper
arranged in
musical array.

He lived
among
thin lines and
built a shelter
between
Earth and

heaven,
playing music
to throbbing
heart beating
rhythms.

He solved a
good and
evil puzzle of
ordinary folks,
faltering and
stumbling
over authentic
notes.

He crossed
judgment lines,
letting
blues music
whisper in
smoke filled
cabarets.

A silhouetted
trumpet player
on a stage in
streaming
flood light haze,
only sought
peaceful
persuasion.

Someday each
must decide
who can step
onto a stage or

not and
who will play
elite blues
and cross
unique lines.

Only a spirit
knowing
own shape
can straddle a
thin wizened
line, and
experience a
lighted
path leading
towards true
expression.

His unique
tortured music
feed souls and
made spirits
shine, and
caused middle
attitude folks to
connect with
those unafraid to
listen.

Music to Dance By

Stand near
flood lights and
allow a sanctuary
blanket to
cover mind,
body and soul.
An enigmatic
world of base,
mid-ranges and
treble produce a
heart pounding
guitar sound.
A good
tomorrow is
remembering
things learned
from yesterday.
Seventies
rock and roll
shakes
hands and
flirts with
destiny yet
today.
Come touch,
swagger and
dance in a
holy place, and
let that
rock music
revive your
hungry soul.

Spiritual Nature

An old spirit
overcomes
negative and
positive with
saintly mid action.
And when loss
meets point of
no return,
it is like a
train half way
home.
It seeks
no station or
hiding place,
but surely
retreats to a
fading middle
place.
However,
there are few
outcomes worth
aspiring for and
destinations worth
driving towards.
Only faith and
righteous spirits
can quell
human nature's
will for
extremes.

Chapter V

Lives

My mother had a professional photograph taken of her and my dad about eight months before he went in the hospital for lung cancer. He never came out alive after about a month of chemotherapy. He died from the chemo.

No one knew he had cancer at the time of this photo, but as I look at it in retrospect, I see that he wasn't well. I see illness in his eyes, but I also see that little grin as if he yet has hopes, dreams and plans for another day or another life.

Fall of 1979

My father was a big man who found pride in his size and physical ability to push, pull and manipulate his physical environment while philosophizing, thinking and reasoning his way through tribulations. I like to think I am much like him in many respects except I never grew as big and I never gained the toughness he possessed.

He developed cancer at the young age of 68 and I never realized how young that was until he was gone, laying in a casket sleeping, appearing as if only 50 years old. Problem is, he was not waking up, not plowing that field during spring time or harvesting that corn during fall.

I helped him harvest his final corn crop just before going into the hospital for chemotherapy to cure the lung cancer. It was a bright sunny day; temperature around forty degrees and the corn was yielding quite well. We both frequently smiled as we enjoyed being together while realizing that harvesting a crop is one of the best of times. It is the reward for working hard at plowing, disking, planting and cultivating while at the same time praying for good weather. Little did we know he would never return to the farm.

He always had plans and dreams, and a positive attitude. I never knew him to quit anything in his life. I had seen him do impossible things like lifting a 2,000-pound hay bailer that had slipped from its jack or seen him solve a mechanical problem with an engine or invent and design a new tool. I had seen him design and construct many things on the farm. I had seen him think and plan his way through life. This situation seemed to be just more of the same. We were both positive. We both had plans.

I remember later sitting in the hospital chapel praying that God would take him easily, would not make him suffer like John D. Turner suffered with cancer. I prayed this because for the first time in my life I began to see retreat in his eyes and lack of resolve. I saw failure in a man who never gave up on anything in his life. I saw a man who had no more plans, dreams or ambition. I cried for him in that chapel for I knew he would not come out of that hospital alive. I prayed that he would not suffer, would maintain his dignity and physical pride, and he did.

My father had always guided me through life with his deep advising voice that I even heard when out in the world alone trying to make a fool of myself and get in trouble. It was like a weight off my shoulders when he died because I became my own man, adviser and planner. I was horribly sad and missed him terribly, but I knew he had suffered only about two days at the end of his hospital stay, and that was not terrible, not like John D. who committed suicide because of all the pain. I became freer after he died, but I could clearly grasp freedom only because he taught me how to be free in the first place.

I yet hear his advising voice and see his physical stature in mind. I play mind movies of him speaking to me, saying those little short advising quotes. I used them much when maturing myself. I used them when educating my son and other young boys. I used them when teaching in middle and high school, teaching boys how to become honest, honorable men.

My mother asked me a couple weeks after his passing if I thought she was crazy by believing that my father had visited her a few days after the funeral. She spoke of being in bed while hearing someone come through the back door, walk to her bedroom, enter and stand over her. She said it was my father and he softly spoke, saying he was fine and for her not to worry. He then turned, walked out of the house, closing the door behind him. I said that I believed her, also thinking that he briefly returned to give advice.

Lessons Taught

A lone petal
among hundreds
seeks another
self-expressed
life day.

Time is simple
among kindred
garden flowers.

Endless
created
unlike plants
wish only
pleasing exist.

Unlike flora
possess similar
aspirations.

Similarity is
common while
understanding
differences is
exceptional.

Plowing

Father and
I plowed
fields for
corn planting.
Windblown dust
burnished
our exposed
sun baked faces.
Roaring exhaust
caused ringing
in our ears.

Deep furrows
hypnotically
guided our
guiding eyes
back and forth
on each side of
laid out lands.
Hundreds of
black birds
trailed plows,
organic earth
worm gathering.

To another land
we went when
soil of one was
fully overturned.
We methodically
plowed first
one then
another land.

Father started a
new land while
I finished an
old one.

He frequently
waved a
meaty hand
"hello" as we
briefly passed
on opposite
land sides.
My smaller
hand returned
his gesture.

A smile often
came over our
tanned faces.
Now and then
he pointed an
index finger,
saying, "hello."
Small gestures
made me feel
loved and
appreciated.

We passed and
met all day long,
playing our little
spring plowing
games.
It was silly
I guess, but
we cherished

every greeting
until work was
completed or
setting sun
signaled us home.

For years this
springtime ritual
continued until
I moved on and
Father stayed with
fields and dreams,
plowing soil and
recalling memories.

I revive those
wonderful times
myself with
mind movies.
I had a great
childhood.
He had a great
fatherhood.

He's gone now,
passed on.
Maybe in heaven
he yet plows,
waves and
smiles as if
it yesterday, and
with greater
clarity than
my here on earth
memories.

Prospecting

I found myself
prospecting for
precious feelings
as if in a stream
gold searching
while leisurely
canoeing mind.

My attention,
reasoning and
reality changed
causing fright as
I suddenly slid
into white water
rushing current.

But, swiftly as
fast water
appeared and
fear invaded,
violent creek
widened and
moved slowly.

I sought fear
no more as
I lay back with
calm mind
while conscious
thought revealed
authenticity.

I silently
surrendered to
reflecting water,
gazing into
own revealing
thoughtful
creek mind.

I saw own
calm moving
water mind
prospecting
in a most
unlikely place,
within myself.

I saw a
golden nugget
in own
shallow mind,
representing
gleaming
courage.

Prospecting
is not difficult
in a shallow,
calm moving
mind and a
brave eye for
golden nuggets.

Revealing Ways

Night speaks
while stars intrigue,
making holes
through heaven to
physically point.

Magnificent stars
visually reveal
rivers murmuring,
trees growing,
winds blustering.

They are spiritual
inhalations, like
divine breaths of
angels divulging
heavenly secrets.

They are God's
edifying hand,
revealing wisdom
with fingers
pointing earthward.

Magnificent stars
visually reveal
earth changing,
man progressing,
humanity learning.

Wheat at Feet

Wheat thrown by a
planting hand
near shoeless
tramping feet causes
spiritual
germination that
stimulates creation.
Golden stalks of
valued souls
soar towards
heaven's realm as
bread after
bread is baked by
mortals seeking
heaven.
God's work is
gentle planting,
grinding and
slowly eating life
while heading
towards a faithful
harvesting point.
To see green
stalks growing,
feel grinding
vibration and
taste warm bread
is purposeful being.
Precious life is like
recycling wheat that
forever nourishes
mankind's seed.

Wisdom Soar

Sharing rain
requires brave
flowers to
seize obedient
sun as if
everything can
see and
hear Spring
articulate
natural seasonal
grace.

When someone
feels another's
caring thoughts
soothing an
impatient mind,
it's like dust
blowing across a
brown pasture,
provoking
willing rain to
feel wanted.

When an eager
mind wishes to
flaunt beauty of an
inspiring thought,
it's like an
impatient spring
flower root
waiting to
fracture and

ascend above
obliging soil.

When natural
enlightenment
eagerly waits for
spirituality to
self speak,
it's like wind and
rain waiting
on cusp of
purity and
faith to cause
blossoming.

When spiritual
wisdom soars
on angel sent
illumination,
it's like a
human being
on tempest edge
waiting for
shining mind and
eager spirit to
flourish.

Heavenly Knowledge

Enlightenment forever seeks.

Weight is a mind felt illusion.

True wisdom is humbling.

Calibrated light portions mind.

Light thoughts pass through space.

Heaven has no standards, only truths.

Heaven's window is small and narrow.

Collected ideas construct imagination.

Souls collect streaming experience.

Birth and death are beginning events.

Pollination has a singular purpose.

Holy Spirit energy permeates everything.

Holy Spirit material is everything.

Old Barn Speaks

Near highway forty-one, a
striking white barn stood
possessing useful dignity.
It found earthen burial as
nature reclaimed material.
It once stood proudly,
straight and beautiful with
painted white board siding,
bright green shingles and
well oiled heavy doors.

I witnessed undoing of
my family farm barn while
driving past a hundred times.
I watched reclaiming and
creative destruction.
Rotted roof sheathing
allowed sun light through
large holes, like haunting
eyes searching sky while
asking, "why me?"

Strong giant hewed beams
held steadfastly together,
seemingly pegged forever,
finally succumbed to
natural weather and gravity.
They clutched remnants while
sticking up through rubble
like defiant broken bones.
Time destroyed all and
laid it away in an artful pile.

Eighteen forty six built
seemed a long existence,
but slow farm death years
became a fast lifetime.
It remarkably got scattered
over crumbled foundation.
Rotting warped boards and
loose shingles got strewn
like sacrificial soldiers and
abandoned machine parts.

One night a selfish man
started a colossal fire,
cremating my barn with
one grand departing act.
It growled and roared
haunting sounds as
I stopped to witness.
I recalled my departed
parents who used that
barn, and I wept.

I remembered people
who crashed and burned.
I well remembered
family and friends falling
in fair and harsh times.
I recalled many souls
bravely passing and
their lifeless bodies
changed by flame into
ash like an old barn.

My Friend Steve

My friend Steve was a
bad ass warrior.
He spent six years in
Viet Nam and Laos as an
Army Green Beret.
He got his hair parted
by a bullet,
shoulder torn up
by a grenade and
his private parts
stabbed with a knife.
He went to every
military school for
self defense so
he could remain alive,
so he said.

He yet fought that war
in mind and heart
after being discharged,
working every day for
prisoners of war.
He couldn't have children,
got divorced after
two married years and
couldn't find a
calm life anymore.
He finally went back
over there secretively to
find MIA prison camps
with no success.
He yet couldn't find a
peaceful mind anymore.

He sold grain bins,
used cars and then
prefab houses, but
he remained a soldier.
He had war equipment
stored in a bedroom.
He had war stored
in his troubled head.
Viet Nam was one place
he truly belonged.
He probably should've
died over there.
He remained ready to
go back to any battle.
He wanted to go to
Desert Storm, but
they didn't need
his kind of fighter.
He couldn't be a
soldier anymore.

He finally died of a
severe heart attack.
He forgot to go to
school and get training
for that silent enemy.
Strange now how
I saw him not too
long before he passed.
Many said he looked good
because he had lost weight.
I thought he looked like
shit because muscle and
strength was severely gone.
He couldn't live a
life anymore.

I should've spoken
because now I know
his heart was not
working correctly.
Steve was a bad ass
warrior, but didn't
know his enemy
lived inside in
more ways than one.
He was uniform
buried at fifty-six with
all his medals.
He will never be a
warrior anymore.

So if you see someone
who looks really well
because they've lost a
lot of weight too fast,
ask them why.
Maybe it's an unseen
enemy creeping
through an
unknown jungle
towards a place with
no self defense.
Maybe it's nothing.
Maybe it's by design.
But just maybe,
it's something that
won't allow
existence anymore.

Grandfather's Tools

Dust collects on
unnoticed tools
laid to rest long ago.
Unused machines sit
idle in dim light of a
woodworking shop.
Grandfather created
family artifacts and
treasures in that
woodworking shop.
His strong hands
sawed, shaped and
fastened wood,
making it behave
like a warrior might
protecting and
defending honor.
Well designed and
skillfully created
furniture sought
attention enough to
withstand time's test.
Grandfather's
furniture remains
useful yet today in
relatives' homes, but
his tools and
machines patiently
wait for a young
woodworker with
artisan skills to make
them valuable again.

Mountain Sought

Blessed are
eagles that
pursue
nature's high
concourse.

Sown within a
willing mind are
creative ideas
silently evolving
like small seeds
deposited in
accruing silt of
eroding rock.

Honorable
journeys begin
up challenging
mountainsides to
retrieve flowers
miraculously
brought to life in
high eagle aeries.

Not just eagles
boldly pursue
brave heights,
but people
also seek
lofty thoughts
like blooming
mountain flora.

Strong young
hands and
capable feet
climb towards
lofty peaks,
and a mind
intuitively seeking
amazing views

Mental silt
sprouts engaging
thoughts and
ideas like
nature grows
flowers out of
thin air and
obliging rocks.

Blessed are
eagles that
pursue
nature's high
concourse.

Weighted Man

Weighty tasks on
my shoulders rest,
pressing downward,
diminishing height.
My diverted eyes
ignore far slopes that
make my climb
more difficult than
fearfully wished or
certainly imagined.

My burdened
round shoulders
carry weight that
seeps and rumples
my worried mind.
Old age creeps and
slowly leaches
bone deep through
thick skin and
throbbing blood.

Hope speaks to a
listening mind
during day and a
haunting soul at
quiet night.
Prayer provides
spiritual relief, and
soon I shall be
weightless and
unencumbered.

Chapter VI

Loves

No matter my age, season or reason, freedom speaks to me with a unique voice. I yet salute my flag and think it is beautiful for in my heart I know liberty gives birth to all other rights, including love, joy and peace.

There always remains some degree of boyish dreams and schemes that will not die, and if they weaken or even disappear, life reminders bring them back. Freedom yet allows my soul to sing and my spirit to dance.

Winter of 1980

When I was very young I had many years to live, but I could not see past present day. I could not imagine what would happen to me in seventy years. Now I am old and can see further into the future, but I will probably not live but a few more years. Strange how two opposites seem to meet in a middle place and become half-way there, but as that center gets nearer and nearer some things increase and some decrease, middle seems to seek itself so as to be balanced. Birth and death are a lifetime apart. Is that statement wisdom or stupidity? For sure it is a dichotomy.

It may take a hundred years to see the truth and maybe even longer to accept the truth, but it only takes one day to know the end is near. I wish I could have seen the future when I was young and I wish I could have the time to be wise now that I am old. I wish I could have shared God's given wisdom when I was young. I wish I could steal youthful time now that I am old.

There is always irony in time and space for each depends on the other to exist just as each life depends on birth and death to exist. Both are a beginning of something. My eyes cannot see what my mind cannot imagine. My imagination cannot return my youth no matter how wise I become.

The irony is within the dichotomy itself, one can only touch and tie both ends of a rope if it becomes a circle, the circle of life, the circle of time. Even when living ties the rope with wisdom and skill, everything lives within and outside the circle. Only God's hangman noose alters all things temporarily. Then, we enter the ultimate dichotomy of heaven or hell.

Somewhere within time and space spent here on Earth, love is found, even if for only a moment, and shared. Most people find many loves in many forms if fortunate during a long life, but if life is short, even for a moment, love is hopefully shared.

There are many different kinds of love that barely touch or penetrate our lives. I have a thousand melancholy thoughts about love and its affect upon me. I sense knowledge about love, but cannot grasp it. I feel as though I am wise about love, but cannot define it. I can only share my interpretation of its existence in my personal time and space. I can only share my experience with its presence and absence, its coming and going, its gain and loss.

I found one of the greatest loves of my life is freedom. I was born free and will die free. Freedom is the beginning of all other loves for it makes possible time and space for a thousand loves. I had no idea freedom was so important when I was young. I could not see past today and tomorrow did not exist when very young. As I got older and started heading for that middle ground of which I have spoken about, I saw freedom expand and unfold before my eyes.

My first felt freedom was being loved by my parents. That never went away. I remember when I got my first car and became mobile. Oh, what freedom I felt and exercised it much. I hate to admit that my freedom and love to drive a vehicle also never left me. My love for Jackie and basketball at seventeen, my love for making love when I was twenty-one and my love for a wife and children at thirty all caused me to mature and gain wisdom about time and space. The love for learning and teaching, the love for accomplishing and succeeding and the love for reward and compensation all gave me security. However, the love for life and living, the process of giving and taking, the love for God's blessings and His love for me is nearly overwhelming. I will not live long enough on Earth to understand His power and grace, but I pray I will be educated in heaven better than on Earth.

Hear Us Purr

Rust on
mind was
like grease-less
gears meshing,
making noise
in a quiet
place where
loud noise was
forbidden.

Out of
fast traffic
I could not
move myself,
could not
drive with
reason or
purpose.

I miraculously
found a
good lady
mechanic
who knew
her stuff and
way around a
mind.

I operated
on seven of
eight
cylinders and
found

she also
on seven.

We remained
together and
cumulatively on
fourteen
cylinders
operated a
wonderful
organic engine.

We soon
learned to
run quietly
on sixteen
cylinders and in a
different artful,
poetic way
we life purred.

Who knew a
good lady
mind mechanic
could restore a
spiritual engine
with a little bit of
love, skill and
knowledge?

Her Claim

A mother's
glean ended
after many
harvest years of
little evidence
as a child
became a
misplaced
wheat grain
among chaff.

She worked to
grind wheat into
hopeful flour
since his birth
like a grist mill
pulverizing, but
on hand and
knee working
yielded little
compensation.

A son's
sinful heart
demanded
kindness and
rejoice as if
she a servant
tending
oven fire while
he rejected
responsibility.

She wept
sour tears and
laid no hope
on intentions
while venders
sold bus
tickets to an
addicted son
begging
false reverie.

Her son
became chaff
to chink a
crack in hell as
heaven refused
redemption
to a deposited
wheat grain
refusing to be
seed or bread.

On Yesterday's Wings

In time rest comes and
seasons fall behind as
I witness beckoning
stars and moon.
My painted portrait is
shredded to potpourri.

Angels build a fire and
fragrant smoke drifts as
cleansing ash and tinder.
They allow fire to reduce
my body to ashes for a
magnificent trip home.

My spirit has served
brain and body well, but
now it feasts on purity
while transporting
precious essence
towards creation place.

My transitional spirit
on guardian angel wings
flies as my old soul in
silver moon light shines
while someone whispers
Earth life approval.

Finding Another

Lonely is when
no one watches
while a partner is
elsewhere, and
when feelings
crush a mind like
fermented grapes
trying to redeem
vineyard history.

As moon light
creeps across
bedroom floor, a
posing mind
imagines more
than should and
whimsical
ideas disarm
common sense.

Truth tugs at
essence like
gravity on a
load as
mind recycles
heavy
reality and
sleep secures
fidelity thoughts.

Time's Reward

Brush hair off
weathered brow,
furrowed from
life encounters.
Feather hand
across cheek,
cause me to
blush and
tell feelings
that expose
myself.
Gaze long,
passionately
then hold
me tightly.
Let night
come quickly
to hide
my bashful
nakedness.
Bathe my
uniqueness with
affirmation.
Consume
my soul with
timid love.
Seek that
place where
we hide,
where tough
times reward.

Simplicity

In moody realm
I search for
simplicity of a
candle as
I difficultly
flounder in
ignorance.

How can a
candle give
little and be
valued much by
songsters and
poets relating
wisdom?

I caress
candle light
at night as
soft external
weakness gives
rise to internal
strength.

Soul buried
knowledge
provides
wisdom like a
waiting arrow
or a lover's
warm lap.

An inner
lighting gift
sets aglow
eyes and face,
then mind and
spirit like a
bonfire.

Candle light
simplicity
untangles
complicated
minds when
baffled by an
ailing world.

As my mood
lingers like a
candle glowing,
I understand
true love
illumines until
last flicker.

Last Candle

I used last match
on last candle and
slept beside her
last time while
fanned air cooled
us one last time.

I now sit like an
Easter Island statue,
half buried in sand,
waiting her return as
divine beings
gather my arms,

They pull me upward
out of sand and
give legs to walk,
to run and then
island explore with
energy and zeal.

I fumble for a
match and candle to
gain a flicker to
lighten my world and
answer a knock at
my front door.

Warrior's Blade

Confidence in
Your voice
I gather and
Feel courage in
In your
Inspiring words.
You perceive
Me not on
Your exodus towards
Self support and
Well being.
You are like a
Warrior's blade
Needing not a
Sheath while
Waiting use.
You do
Not flash
Threaten or
Rebel.
When brief
Mutiny subsides
In misty
Morning haze,
You will hand an
Olive branch.
You need not
Victory poise,
But only a
Loving place to
Belong.

Zero to Sixty

My life was applied
zero to sixty, then
lazy eighty while
driving at sixteen.

Rules were difficult
when young filled with
accelerated straights,
weaves and slides.

My first velocity taste
was wonderful, but
good to last drop
didn't apply well.

Life teased mind as
I accelerated from
calm to wow, then
unveiled temptation.

I was impatient and
learned to motor
recklessly with an
intense attitude.

By twenty-one
I journeyed on
anywhere roads,
speedometer ignorant.

Strawberry Wall Paper

Do opportunities diminish with time and
how many ticks does a clock possess?

o

An old electric
clock hanging
on a strawberry
papered
kitchen wall
when ten
years old is much
different than a
battery operated
oak clock
hanging on a
painted sheetrock
kitchen wall when
sixty years old.

Ideas soared as
opportunities
tantalized and
imagination raged
when I was young.
But, unlike a clock
I sought success and
ignored passing
time for fifty years.
I didn't count seconds,
minutes and hours.
Time seemed forever.
I stood still while

time passed.
That ticking sound
later haunted
limited dreams and
lost opportunities.

I finally realized
that boyish allure
in tattered psyche
yet existed as
I recalled strawberry
papered walls and
childhood dreams.
I needed to escape
from good behavior,
hard work and
nagging reasonability.

I began picking
strawberry dreams
again discovered
in that kitchen at
that youthful time.
I began appreciating
silent digital clock
time swiftly passing.
I luckily learned that
time is priceless and
clocks have purpose.

o

To whom am I responsible and
how many beats does a heart possess?

Time Doesn't Matter

Walls bring only
fleeting hope
while castles soar
confidently in
passing time.

Citadels that
render grandeur
can be destroyed
in a minute or a
thousand years.
Travelers evaluate
magnificent bridges
frequently or with a
momentary glance.
Paths that begin and
end at water's edge
cannot explain
their gained or
lost presence.
People perpetually
measure passing
time momentarily.

Fraudulent time
has no height,
depth or width, but
is deceptively
momentous.

Inches Apart

We sat inches apart
saying nothing,
gazing through
windshield while
asphalt slid
beneath and
countryside
passed beyond
open windows.
Bright sunlight and
engine hum
caressed our minds.
We simultaneously
pulled down
own sun visors.
We were
speechless
in comfortable
silence.
Conversation was
needless while
knowing inward
thoughtfulness
meant
understanding.

Chapter VII

Times

I can honestly say that this guitar helped save my life, for I was alone in a pit with no help in sight except for God, and He said, "Start climbing." I bought this beautiful Yamaha solid wood guitar and taught myself how to pluck with three fingers and a thumb. I wrote my own songs and sang many of them a few times in public.

She became my lover, Zen master and mental crutch. I seldom play her anymore. I just gaze at her and remember how she saved my mind from havoc and despair. I put my poetry in books now, but I yet hear those melancholy rhythms in my head.

Spring of 1982

I was coaching girls varsity basketball when my tenuous marriage fell apart due to circumstances seemingly beyond my control. I think I and my first wife were very different when we got married and she changed little and I change much. Our core personalities never changed. She was extremely cautious of life and I wanted to embrace it. I welcomed change, especially if being in some control of it, and thus I was not afraid of taking prudent chances.

I also became afraid of the world after having two children, and feeling the pressure of providing for and keeping them safe. I, with her influence, finally got to a point where it was even scary to drive on the highway. Don't get me wrong, she was and is a fine person and I cannot speak badly about her; it is just that I became something that I did not like. I became a person afraid of life.

I lost that youthful attitude I once employed to most everything I attempted. I yet have a bit of boy within me, even at seventy years of age, and hope I will never relinquish it. I disliked my life more and more with passing time. I originally thought that marriage and life in general was as it seemed to be. I thought most everyone settled down, became boring and afraid of change.

I discovered that I was wrong when I began coaching the girls varsity basketball team at Crawfordsville High School. I saw in those young women a sense of discovery and a need for adventure. Together, we thought anything was possible. Two seasons were challenging as they listened to me and I developed and solidified my life philosophy through the game of basketball. The third season was painful as I became anxious and depressed. I became that two sided coin people talk about. I had developed my basketball philosophy from several years of coaching boys basketball from seventh to ninth grade, but being head varsity coach also demanded a definite philosophy to accomplish goals and succeed in life. The girls and I spent a great deal of time together and I saw in them the same attitude I once possessed.

I needed my youthful, fearless attitude back. I wanted to tackle the world in more ways than coaching and teaching. I wanted to kick some ass and needed to find another time, place and person with whom to do it. Between personal desires to express myself, coaching the girls who had freedom and courage, and finding myself in a marriage with a person who did not wish to take chances, I began a downward spiral into a pit of despair.

I found myself in a black hole with no way out except to go inward and retreat from everything. I finally got to a point where I was in that black hole mentally looking for a gun. I had faint ideas of ending it all, but never took myself seriously. I had put myself in a place where no one would come and be with me except God. I finally heard God say. "See that pin point of light up there, climb towards it and I will help you out of this pit."

I began to climb out of that pit as the season ended and I started writing poetry again, putting my thoughts and philosophy on paper. I went to Lafayette and bought a three-quarter guitar, then slowly taught myself how to play it. I moved up to a regular size, solid wood guitar, and began writing and singing my own songs. That guitar was part of the saving of me.

I finally got a gig, after auditioning for my friend Jan Cook who had to hide under a coffee table to listen to me because I was embarrassed to sing and play for anyone. She got me a gig at a local bar and had a contract signed by Sue Key, who owned the bar, on a napkin. I think we all took it as a joke at first, but I got serious about having courage enough to perform before an audience, to share my feelings and world-expose my true self.

I forced myself to play and sing before that first audience. It was hell and I sweated bullets, but I did it. I rigged up a sound system, got a microphone and an electronic pick-up for my guitar. My first gig paid $50. I played one set three times because that was all the material I had memorized. I think no one noticed me at first because I was like background music. I sang only a few other times, wrote a bunch of songs and recorded one tape. I yet have that tape somewhere. That was my musical career.

I had a man tell me one night when I was singing that he also wrote songs, but they were home in a drawer somewhere. I promised myself immediately that I would not leave my songs in a drawer, just as I hopefully won't leave my poems in a drawer. Good, bad or indifferent, I write my thoughts and put them into books.

I went on to get a divorce. I found out what real pain is when I left my children behind. I cried most every night for a few months, then every few nights and then just once in awhile because I missed living with my children. I learned not to cry for many years until life events demanded it, and I could not help myself. Some things in life just break our hearts and crying is about all we can do. I saw my children, Brook and Kristen, a couple times a week, but I just missed being with them and living with them. I eventually was not in the pit and I got somewhat contented with my life.

I went on to do many other things in my life. I was not afraid to take chances and follow my desires with courage. I exercised my freedom of mind, soul and spirit. I yet allow that boyish part of me to exercise liberty.

Freedom Flow

I straddle soft
motorcycle seat,
watching world
pass before eyes in
freedom mind state.

Vague troubles
eclipse mind as
careless wind
slip streams body.
Paint and chrome
catch notice as
throbbing engine
wisdom speaks.

Whole machine
Zen hums,
teaching
unity and
triviality,
disarray and
order as
moment ever
blends.

I count
middle road
stripes passing
beneath feet.
Asphalt grips
small tire surface,
keeping reality
straight upright.

A fractional
amount of
earth connected
soft rubber
tires securely
grip as
thin metal
spokes
support speed,
distance and
inertia at
seventy miles
per hour.

Approaching riders
victory wave,
riding from
unknown places.
All is right in
mind and
body as
security seeks
own destiny.
Sun and
wind bathe
body and
soul.
I balance
earthly motion as
heart sings.

Reasoning scrubs
thoughts and
answers come
easily,
bringing

life security
bits and
pieces.
I conclude,
safety is
illusion,
balancing is
inertia,
remaining
upright and
straight is skill.

Doubt doesn't
threaten
grasping mind,
glancing eyes,
aware ears and
controlling hands.
I approach
unknown world
with both
trepidation and
confidence.
I live to ride and
ride to live.

Life Zen hums,
teaching unity,
triviality,
disarray and
order as every
moment blends.

Silence

Speak no more
aging mouth for
wisdom there
never found a
home, and
like a failed
gold mine's
cave mouth,
no value left
through its
pathway flows.

Surely now
I listen to
wisdom and
let stupidity and
tranquilly brush
my mind.
Birds now sit
on shoulder and
grass grows
beneath
my silent feet.

o

Let silence
bake bread and
daily feed a
gentle soul
that has
little to say.

Trust

An enlightening
glimpse of
loving trust,
caught in a secret
mind place,
grew brighter
minute by minute.
I discovered
stars within a
soul suitcase.
I opened it, and
in eyes,
face and spirit
sweet trust shined.
It was unexpected,
appearing like
something
out of eye corner.
It seized
my attention as
might a
flowing breeze
brush face or
reflecting sunlight
surprise eyes.
Suitcase stardom
shined, and
I felt
graceful Trust
get placed in
awkward hands.
She whispered
words that

soaked my
gathering soul
like a waiting
spring rain.
I accepted
Trust as
strength enough
to defend
planting seeds,
growing flowers,
picking fruit.
And from
my gathered
soul suitcase,
I pulled
Trust and
forever carried
her in mind with
faith, hope and
confidence.
My world
flourished.

Wheat

Some wheat
grains are
scattered,
left on a
stone bed to
sleep, dry,
die or
be wind
brushed like
strewn souls.

Some wheat
grains
might be
planted in
fitting soil,
left to grow
deep
roots that
reach for
knowledge.

Most wheat
grains,
however,
mature into
thousands or
get miraculously
thrashed,
ground and
baked into
life bread.

Loving

When loving
turns to love as
Spring to
Summer, nearly
without notice,
it invites amiable
wisdom of how
nature grows and
affection reaps.
A kiss, touch or
look can feed a
soul without
preparing meals,
stirring pots or
even slicing bread.
Loving has
turned to love
when old hands
hold old hands
on a golden
leafed trail
through a quiet
park on a
rejoicing life
Fall day.

Man In Paradise

I see no place here or
there making sense in
passing ignorant time.
Shadows glide slowly
while wind blows
her chiffon dress.
It brushes my face
with an indirect touch
while I sit admiringly.
I wish to love here in
summer's leisure with
flying hair in warm sun.
Time seeks me out
like a mad soldier at dusk
needing a sleeping place.
I wish that soft dress
against my face again, but
angry time will not allow
another day in paradise.
I seek no glory, revenge,
fame or fortune,
only a women's love.
I call to her when
shadows fade to blackness,
moon-light reflects and
surf foam disappears.
I walk along our beach
one more time thinking,
whispering her name and
wishing her ever near for
I know tomorrow will
steal her presence and
erase our paradise.

Many Love Poorly

Many love poorly
like sprinkling rain,
seemingly valuable
while meaninglessly
leaving soil wanting.
Pretending adore is
only surface felt,
briefly consumed and
pointlessly shallow,
like drops on
hot dusty soul
needing a
good soaking of
positive assurance.

Honest love
encourages upward
reaching roots as
genuine actions
eliminate mistrust and
foster true expression.
Soaking love
drenches assurance,
saturates certainty and
drives roots deeply
towards earthen grace
where purity flows,
security unites and
loving spirits live.

Morning Light

I see hopeful
morning light
through window
warm accumulating
on humble home
belongings.

I eat cereal,
drink coffee and
watch TV sitting
in my overstuffed
obliging chair as
morning expands.

Day becomes
heat weighty as
time passes and
circumstances
become reality
beyond control.

Bright day
turns hot and
threatening as
worrisome night
cannot arrive
fast enough.

I ask
when did
I last lay
relaxed and
quietly alone
with another?

A few
mornings ago,
seems a
life time ago,
I whisper to
only myself.

Back aches,
eyes wilt, but
in quiet
darkness
my tranquil
grin exists.

I put
myself to
bed only to
wait for
morning
sunlight.

I feel
feathers under
head as
mind drifts
into wanted
slumber.

Now Is Then Again

A love song
reflects a melody
remembered
from self history.
Melancholy
pictures fill
my head like an
intentionally
placed album as if
time speaks and
history teaches.
Feelings that
once were are
now again.
I see my past as
it once was and
wish it again.
My heart seeks
too much and
mind remembers
too well.
I cannot relive or
revive my past,
so I now
only hum a
reflected song
to a muffled
melody
created during a
seemingly
obsolete time.

Sacrificial Fulfillment

Confidently a
brown rose bush
middle stands in
chilly woodland
shadows.
Wholly something
special is going to
occur as
nature's secret
genealogy code
is about to
validate Spring.

Time brings
life and
begets fruit
with a tranquil,
disciplined touch.
Cold rain
alters earth and
washes small
new leaves
clinging to life.
New briers
burst to serve as a
natural defense.

Flourishing bush
rejoices as
sunlight speaks
it further into
existence, and
through some

unknown ability,
abundant life
expands and
spreads as if
reaching for
help beyond
anchoring roots.

It seems to
gaze skyward,
knowing a
higher power
chooses life.
Glory stretches
limits as
soil fuels
determination
during
anxious weeks.
Small pink
flowers burst
into being and
aroma fills
woods with
promise.

Mother patiently
waits for
everything and
then temporarily
lays down
her precious
calendar.
She casually
allows self
consumption as

her natural
genetically coded
faith guides
every planned
life progression.

Like a
rose bush,
everything gains
natural essence
through
coded existence.
Everything
possesses
precious emergent
knowledge and
thus natural
purpose.

Silently Waiting

When rain
comes to a
place where
rain is seldom,
it makes
news.
When life
is taken
in a place,
believed
safe,
it makes
news.

I sit on a
campus bench
silently waiting
humanity,
wondering
why I am
in such a
civilized place.
Rape,
murder and
pillage
do not
exist here.

My Worn Rock and Roll Ears

I think of days when
confidence grew and
possibility had
no end; when
youthful ignorance and
false pride was
somehow wonderful.
Sun drenched
my long flying hair as
I traveled fast over
smooth roads that
made my youthful
mind spin, and
seek faster and
faster highway
exploits.
My hot rod pipes
rattled obnoxious
ambiance and
glorious thoughts
rattled my brain.

I could clearly see
my dust with
dawn soaked eyes as
I invaded a
waiting world that
hated change.
I could hear
music blaring in
delicate ears
wishing to close a
thick door between
society and me.

I ask has anything
changed, am
I not you now again?
I hear that
awful music and
see speed breaking
today's highways.
Time alters
tomorrow's view of
truth and justice.
I wish I could
close that door
now myself;
instead, I will join
your party and
dance my own
dusk dance to
your music.
That is if I can
hear with my worn
rock and roll ears.

Chapter VIII

Thoughts

Those two little girls gave me the greatest highs and lows of my life. God gives and takes away, but doing it so dramatically to me, just didn't seem fair.

One week I had everything and the next week everything was destroyed by the death of my sweet Kaitlyn Marie. I eventually also lost Angela Lea, even though yet alive, she is not in my life. I miss them both horribly.

Spring of 1991

My twin daughters were born on March 29 in the Neonatal Intensive Care Unit of Methodist Hospital at Indianapolis. They came into the world premature at thirty-two weeks. Kaitlyn was 3 lb, 7 oz and had to remain in the ICU for about two weeks and Angela was 3 lb, 2 oz and had to stay about a month. They had to weigh 4 pounds before allowed to leave the hospital. They were both healthy, complete in every way and beautifully alike.

I could hold either one of them in one hand. I wept many times when with them in that holy place where life and death silently resides, where parents pray and thank God every day and where dedicated doctors and nurses accomplish miracles. I was no different than most people, recognizing the holiness of the ICU and angels all about. I did not know the power of the Holy Spirit at that time and did not accept the power of God in those days. I recognized God's work, but did not know his influence on and in my life.

Those two little girls were the beginning of my renewed spiritual education. They were my teachers immediately, matter of fact, they continued to teach me as they got older and Kaitlyn yet teaches me from the grave. Kaitlyn died of streptococcus A bacteria at age three and a half years. I wrote about the whole ordeal and thus many repercussions in my book, Letters to Angela. I will say here and now, however, that her passing changed everything in my life. I found the Holy Spirit and purpose for my life beyond what I thought possible.

Her passing caused me to begin seriously writing my thoughts, feelings and emotions in a form of giving and receiving information. Her passing caused me to find my Moses stick, as I call it, and that Moses stick being my writing. Good, bad or indifferent, my writing is what it is.

For those who have not experienced the loss of a child, no matter what age, cannot understand the physical, emotional and mental pain one must endure. My heart was literally broken and my mind literally torn to shreds. It took me a long time to recover and getting a second divorce didn't help.

My wife and I never touched again except for one spurious good-bye hug. She began a parental alienation program almost immediately and I finally lost Angela as a result of her mother's apparent dislike of me. I never judged her or made accusations. Maybe she could read my mind.

I only share here in this chapter some thoughts because of my awful pain, truth discovery and joy for the Lord. I only wish to express some ideas and philosophy that may or may not be useful to someone else. I truly do realize my blessings. It is just a bit difficult sometimes to express what I know and feel. Wisdom is a tough teacher and writing is an emotional profession. I write best alone while Lazy Boy sitting in a dim room while blues music listening and laptop word composing.

Mental Travail

I dreamed of
being carried on
wayward wind.
Doubts floated
below like
clouds meeting
destiny and
finding a
home within
my turbulent
mind.

I saw stacked
imagined barriers
falling like
pillows off a bed,
dropping to a cold
wooden floor,
knowing no other
place to be.

Pragmatic words
echoed in mind,
warning loudly.
Crashing
swords killed
ideas on a
battlefield of
lost causes.
All that was
desired
on that cold
gloomy day was

warmth,
attention and
respect.
Wind yet
chilled and
clouds caused
doubt,
destiny was
murky.

I finally
realized that
barriers were
like soft pillows,
words were not
swords and
tomorrow
would not
be so difficult.
Destiny
would not be a
stormy mental
travail.
I was glad
it was all a
dream wrapped
in suspicion.

Pablo

Please push
my awareness,
give one word,
speak a sentence to
spark my interest
in rebellious
poetic action.

Let me hear a
sweet story or
taste a
bitter joke.
Let me sense
your enigmatic
nature.

Let me walk a
Chilean shore,
see green sea and
read passionate
love poems
in more than
ten letters.

I am drawn
towards
Easter Island
where spirits
speak
louder than
either of us.

I find more
than words in
your poetry,
more than
thoughts to
provoke
gut reaction.

Let me sing
your songs that
never got written,
breathe fresh air
not so long ago
you breathed and
fostered words.

Come sit beside
my mind,
help me be more
than I am and
let me be
something near
what you were.

We have no
mind limits as
I seek ghostly
wisdom and
empathy from a
man who knew
many secrets.

Perimeters

Mass has
little meaning
until a perimeter,
outline or
termination is
noticed and
studied.
Object shape
gives meaning to
existence.
Thin defining
lines separate
mass into form.
Everything is
unseen until
shape is
defined by
limits.
Everything is
separated by
thin lines that
disappear into
mass.
Sooner or later,
everything is a
silhouette begging
exposure by an
able limitation.
Everything is
fine line
defined by
enlightenment.

Shoe Soles

Soles of my shoes have soul and a
Unique private place to be while
I travel rebellious Earth.
My soles carry me onward and
Protect me from abusive distractions.
A harsh world seeks intrusion as
My soles gather earthen stain while
Dust and rain are repelled.
An ignorant life collects and serves, and
Knows no limits to discomfort and pain.
Each shoe I put away at night
Rests and cautiously waits for
Tomorrow, and a new adventure.
Brilliance examines itself by
Putting new imprints on Earth and
Connecting soles to new paths.
Soulful soles tell many stories as
Time seeks their demise.
Life is shoe sole analogous and
I am sole soulful, and not
afraid to step forward.
No other can walk in my shoes or
Employ my unique soul.

I Yet Mind Cruise

I was caught between
fantasy and reality,
too healthy and
young to conform.

Seems age matters and
dreams can go blind.
I carelessly left
many days behind.

I slow cruised on a
Hawaiian beach in
my fifty-seven Chevy
surfer wagon.

Numbered days and
cost of living said "no."
World opinion and
age revealed truth.

I loved my dreams,
thinking them heavenly,
then shadows gathered
them into night.

Down near Kailua Beach
I yet observe,
bright surf boards and
wind kites riding high.

I surely loved
my dreams,
thinking heaven sent,
but earthly found.

Mind Seams

I thought days of
wilderness seeking had
melted away into
time and space,
no more passing
my leisure window
from where I sat
watching limited
myopic views of
what life could be and
had sorely become.
Yet in span of
long lived time
reclusive dreams
returned to an
old man, and
replaced laziness with
spirited grace that
brought back and
sewed doubtful
mind seams torn.
A dream cloak again
wrapped my body,
mind and soul, and by
grace of God
I discovered
another window
through which to see a
new wilderness, and
seek a rebuilding of
time and space at
my leisure.

Three Feet Away

Insecurity is an
eighteen wheel
Mack truck
cruising down
Interstate Seventy at
eighty miles
per hour with
over loaded steel
heading for
some factory
with a running late
sleepy man
on eye opening
speed drugs
behind a big
steering wheel with
peddle to metal
who has
heart-burn from
fat and sugar
filled food for
dinner,
listening to
rock and
roll music
passing three feet
away from
my oncoming
car door.

Lucky

Gathering storm
threatens as
sunlight wanes and
trees wind whisper.

I think and
feel safe as
thunder moans as
disaster groans.

I'm lucky for
tragedy goes West,
around me and
doesn't touch.

I'm lucky that
tears don't
fill my eyes and
cancer is dead.

But, how long can
good luck run and
safe probability
cards not change?

I can only attempt
ignorance of
black clouds
threatening calm.

Kite Dreams

Night dreams
float in my mind with
delicate ease as if
controlled with
harassing strings.
Those images are
like kites warm air
managing a windy sky.
My mind fears
calm and truth will get
recklessly replaced.
Control is beginning to
feel like scattered
Fall leaves haphazardly
seeking solid ground.
My mind begins to
paint wispy answers
describing and
picturing, but
not explaining, and
will not define
puzzling views.
My artful mind flies on
whispering wind
when asleep, but
defies meaning
when awake.
My dreams disappear
into momentary skies
like kites released from
controlling strings.

How Far

Wise stars
shed vital light
above a
crooked river and
seem to appear
as if on an
ever journey of
knowing self.

A wise river
flows and
learns to
meander
through
choice mazes of
least resistance
towards an
unknown end.

An ignorant
firefly
knows not
he cannot light a
world, but a
moon
knows how
much there
is to illumine.

A man is like a
winding river and a
divine star,
he knows not

flow distance,
yet knows there
is much to learn
about cosmic
flowing.

An old man's
wisdom soaks
his mind
only after
knowledge
is gathered,
grapes are
harvested and
wine is sipped.

Stars and
rivers teach, but
only if light and
water are
studied with
sober minds and
clear spirits
focused on
humanity.

While Time Is Friendly

Near silence
prevails with
calm sea and
little wind
today while
I walk timid
sandy shore.
Pelicans skim,
dolphins surface,
my environment
triumphs as
I acquiesce to a
higher power,
hearing peace,
feeling tranquility.
Cloudy sky
frames horizon as
hidden sunlight
struggles to penetrate.
Time disappears
in my head as
life touches
my heart like
tiny waves
lapping shore.
I feel grateful,
whispering
short prayers,
realizing grace
penetrates self.
Nothing changes
except me as
I do nothing.

Oh, how quickly
Earth can
change with
mighty natural
forces, with
power and
intimidation.
Today
this calm,
windless sea is
static, yet
deeply
changing me.
It subtly alters
my mind and
disposition with
bird wings,
dolphin splashes,
breeze brushes and
sunlight coloring.
Nature penetrates
brain and body
through senses.
God remakes
my mind
through love and
obliging time.

Thoughts Howl

Thoughts often
howl through a
natural mind like
aggressive wind
threatening sanity,
roaring like a
rampaging tornado
changing everything.

Thoughts can rip
mental castles and
shanties alike, but
when calm resides,
whole self feels
safe with middle
reasoning and
balanced sense.

Preferred thoughts
cerebral float like
spiritual clouds and
whispering poems,
sweeping and
cleaning castles and
shanties alike of
vicious psychosis.

Chapter IX

Processes

I wish my cremated body ashes be put in a small well-crafted oak box like Kaitlyn's and placed in either a plot with a modest headstone or a columbarium niche with a small brass name plate, which ever seems logical to those left behind.

I don't regret living with some pain and suffering, but enjoy more the times with love and joy. Don't worry about me, I have spiritually considered the greatest dichotomy, and have chosen Heaven over Hell and know how to get there.

Winter of 1991

My mother died a few weeks after Christmas of 1991. She went to the beauty parlor to get her hair fixed, came home and died that night. A neighbor found her the next morning and said she had a pleasant look on her face while yet in bed. She was seventy-nine years old, and still had a wonderful attitude and a youthful outlook on life.

She was about five feet tall, but seemed taller than that when I was ten years old. I thought I was tall at ten, not realizing she was short at thirty-seven. I thought I was a real man at that time, being big and ignorant for my age.

My father was six feet four, two-hundred and sixty pounds. I yet do not understand how I failed to correlate my size according to his size. I guess he was just unusually large and beyond real magnitude comprehension for a little admiring son.

I laid my Mommy to rest on a week day afternoon. I very much was a little boy when saying good-bye to her at the funeral home even though I was fifty-two. It is strange how we are all "momma's boys" when push comes to shove and life seems a bit overwhelming. My mother Louise was a powerful little woman that gained my respect with the help of my father who provided a good example concerning how to be an honorable respectful man.

I never saw my parents argue or even hotly debate anything. They always seemed to agree. I guess there are a million processes that take place in a person's life, but the process of marriage surely is one of the hardest and possibly the most long lasting. They say now days that the average marriage lasts about seven years. My parents were married about forty-seven years.

I have had three marriages lasting twelve and seven years and working on a third one now six years. I am no example of a marriage process man. Truthfully, I am not a good example for hardly anything. I, however, can

189

draw contrasting images of good and bad, right and wrong, and success and failure. That surely provides some positive examples somehow.

I keep looking at the great role models I had with my parents, figuring some things just did not rub off. I have a dichotomy working in my head about what is good and correct in a marriage. My first marriage was my fault. I will take the majority of blame for its demise for I had ideas, dreams and ambitions beyond my first wife's realm.

The second was partially my fault because I had no business marrying such a younger woman. I do not know why she married me after living with me for several years. She told me later that she never loved me and that she married me to escape from her family in Florida. Whatever her reason, everything and every possibility of marital success crashed around us when our daughter Kaitlyn died. The marriage had no chance of survival from that moment onward.

I don't blame God at all and never got angry with Him for taking Kaitlyn at such a young age. I think Jesus took her back to heaven so that she wouldn't suffer horribly later in life. Angela, her twin sister, suffers from several medical conditions. I guess Kaitlyn's conditions would have been worse.

The process of living with pain and suffering is a mystery and comes in many forms. I have touched the extremes of life, suffered pain and found joy along the way. I have learned to process life through reasoning and thinking, feeling and expressing, living and dying.

The dichotomies of life haunt me with melancholy memories. I, however, consider myself one of the lucky ones and have physically suffered little, but have mentally suffered the worst thing that can happen to a person, death of a child. I know the contrast of many processes.

Silent Sunset

Oh, red sunset
you gradually change and
silently surrender light to
consuming darkness.

No insightful words
can reconcile
night treachery that
causes day demise.

To mislay so much
without moan,
groan or whimper
makes a heart ache.

Yet relentless time
renews morning and
again and again
resurrects glorious day.

So be still heart for
morning amiably
caresses night like
mind seeks wisdom.

Another precious day
will not ignore life,
unless a spirit says
good-bye before dawn.

Seeds

Life cycles
begin and
end with
mid gathering
event flow as
awareness
glues spiritual
returning to
heaven
transitional
material
together.

Life creates,
stores and
transports
seeds in a
magnificent
universe with
spiritual care
like plants
preserve
ending and
germinate
beginning seeds.

Life, however,
might soar
from here to
there in
streaming
middle
grace as if

all essence
evolves and
never truly
commences or
concludes.

Scholars and
theologians
lecture and
preach, but
they don't
know how a
magnificent
cosmos begins or
ends as
evolution seeks
ever-lasting
graceful life.

Everyone is a
wilting,
dying plant
losing leaves and
holding seeds,
preparing to
soar a familiar
path towards
heaven and
no one here
knows how or
why.

My Watch

Time wishes to
be left alone,
sulking in favor of
strangers, not
looking my way or
measuring for me.

It's bound in a
little sphere with
bold numbers and
thin hands that
maneuver me
through space.

It's strapped to
my wrist with a
thin black leather
piece of cow hide
serving as taken life
without notice.

I find no solace in
time's hypocrisy,
pretending to care,
pretending not
complicit in bad
ill-timed events.

I observe time
watch move, but
do not realize
its true passing,
process or
intelligence.

It ticks in ears,
silently controls,
clutches to
sweaty wrist as
morning seeps and
evening weeps.

It's an
old simple watch and
I can't imagine
anything more
complicated than
gears and a spring.

I then realize it is
I who sulks,
wishes to be
left alone and
cannot count ticks
echoing in ear.

It is I
who kills cows,
assembles
mechanical parts and
straps time to
my failing body.

I finally
discover that
it is I who can save
much life time by
removing my useless,
haunting watch.

Helpless

A robin built her nest
near a back door,
laid four eggs and now
sits there nearly all day
until a door opens or a
near cat follows intrigue.
She then abandons
her nest swiftly,
chattering and warning,
but everyone knows
she's helpless to defend
nest, eggs or even herself.
She's like a helpless
rabbit also not far
from that back door.

Even most helpless
humans chatter and
swear as if defending
themselves against
impending danger.
There's always
someone stronger,
tougher and meaner;
always something scary
lurking in shadows that
makes people anxious.
There's always a noisy,
scary door creaking
some place near a
back door.

Hidden Gift

In covert places
secrets hide,
hidden from
ordinary search.
Once I played
hide and seek.
Now it is not a
game I play with
those wishing
disclosed truth.
Emotions and
passions
delicately settle as
mind shadows
hide in
crevassed repose.
Strong doors are
locked with
keys available
only for myself.

My friend
burned down
his mind and
all was lost.
It's a mystery to
where he took
all those secrets.
Now angels
play his game,
for he lives
with them now.

Created secrets

sooner or later
consume secret keeper.
Secrets kill and
burn down minds.
As for me,
I cannot afford
reconstruction or
mending materials.
Time is precious,
labor costs are
skyrocketing and
my energy is
dwindling.
I'm too old for
new game
learning and
old game
burning.

Sooner or Later

Can you hear
my pounding heart
yielding to
blemishing anxiety?
Can you hear
my low mind murmur
while seeking
unwilling answers?
My spirit
mumbles as if
unfamiliar
questions and
answers
will not
share life's rejoice.
Sleep is an
enemy lurking and
will not appear.
Morning can
come not
soon enough for
only then can
life's challenges
be addressed.
Sooner or later
my body will
relent to
lacking energy.
Sooner or later
morning will
diminish night and
I'm afraid my spirit
will not be ready.

Old Beauty

Our old bricks lie
mortared with
composed essence,
waiting destruction.
We are three storey
buildings of
form and function.
Time was easy
before wary decay.
Skyscrapers here
now surround,
leaving us like
wilting flowers that
used to flourish.

Someone is
needed to
stack and
hold, and be
willing and able to
surely appreciate
worthy repair.
Young architects
look at us with
puzzling eyes and
short lived minds, and
judge old values
from a different
point of view.

Sun ignores us
old brick buildings
sitting among

taller and more
modern edifices of
smooth skin design.
We are clothed with
mortared bricks of
rough outer essence.
We have not lost
our zest and
grace, and that
which made this
city first eminent

Let not our
obscurity dwell for
our likeness will
not come again.
Those new shiny
metal and glass
skyscrapers reflect
God's face, but
we as old, obsolete,
obscure buildings
absorb His grace and
keep it safe within
our self-proclaimed
spirit and soul.

Tall Trees

I walk among
passive trees
leaf clothed
in summer, but
now winter
naked.
They brazenly
stand as if being
voyeurs watching
me watch them.
Some stand
confidently while
others struggle.
Is a forest of
transient trees
different than
my fellow
human beings?
Strong ones
sky reach,
while weak ones
survival fight.

Everything and
everyone faces
natural passing
like a tree,
hoping for a
wearing away
through maturity.
Weather fails,
wind splits,
drought robs as

time kills.
Each season
dances
over and
beneath
would be
graves, and
only God
knows
falling time.

Hopefully
I will fall
while sun,
moon and
stars
yet cast
shadows with
my leafy
bulk or
perhaps
I'll be
altered into
useful or
donated
parts, but
I fear
saw teeth
will gnaw at
my heart and
make my sap
flow.

Sound of Spring

Mystic sense of
sound compels
my heart to sing.
Dawn brings
water falling and
rainbows seeking to
alter my mood.
New temptations
flower reward for
no one predicted
last winter's
resulting
strength.

Nature seeks,
finds and
Spring displays.
She provokes
hearing minds and
feeling hearts to
beauty advance.
She well teaches
listens and
learns, and
believes in
own mystical
power.

Chapter X

Realizations

After suffering the worst that could happen to me, everything else seems easy. Oh, I sometimes feel sorrow and pain, but it fades with a consoling spirit in my heart, mind and soul.

As an awesome sunset closes an old day, another sunrise opens a new glorious day on Earth for me. I am a spiritual being passing day by day time until I go back home.

Fall of 1994

Some events leave a wound forever. I have a scar so deep it yet hurts when recalling how it got there and the pain endured receiving it. It seems like only yesterday in some ways and a lifetime in other ways. I play vivid movies in my head about a September morning when Kaitlyn died in a Crawfordsville, Indiana hospital. I write about her passing in a book entitled, Letters to Angela, giving details and a time line that will not satisfy absence, history or suffering. She was only three and a half years old, but lived a lifetime of influence. She was spiritual in many life aspects, sharing her spirituality without knowing it, being an angel without knowledge of heaven. She changed everything for me when she died and went to heaven.

Her twin sister, Angela, witnessed Kaitlyn in heaven by Jesus allowing a short visit immediately after her passing. Angela shared a little bit of her heavenly knowledge and meeting Jesus with me. I need no further proof than a three and a half year old child witnessing to me. She said that Jesus spoke to her and said, "I accept you." What more can one ask, but to know Jesus accepts you. I yearn for those three words or even that one word, "accepts."

I believe God has spoken to me twice in my life. The second time was when I was out in the woods by myself trying to make sense of Kaitlyn's death. God told me, "Be grateful for the time you had with her. She was a blessing while here." I followed His advice and accepted the help of the Holy Spirit. I have peace concerning her passing, but am yet frequently sad and heartbroken. I relate to people who have lost a love one and if time and place permits, I try to console them. I encourage them to keep an open mind for possible contact with the passed spirit. I had five spiritual encounters with Kaitlyn and I appreciate them yet today for they gave me closure and understanding. They are precious memories for me. I have always wished for one more contact, but that has not happened. I still keep an open mind and heart for such a wonderful event to again occur.

I appreciate the knowledge that I have people up there waiting for me when it is my time to go to heaven. I recognize the so called beginnings and endings in all aspects of my life, but have come to believe that there are no real endings, but only transitions when it comes to life and death. There are only endings here on Earth. Therefore, when the spirit of God is in a child of God, there is no real ending. I pray that I will experience this transition and pass quietly in the night like my mother. If that is not possible, let me go shortly in the morning like Kaitlyn. If that is not possible, then let me pass willingly in a few painful days like my father.

Crushed Leaves

Crushed leaves
on a black
topped road,
ground into
brown small
particles lay
deadly silent.
I walk past and
on them, and
in their
worthless state
I see my own
ground past
as if being
those leaves.
But, in one
relating moment
I am walking
towards
my future,
leaving historical
mind behind and
embracing a
new mind.
I am as if a
naked tree
waiting patiently
for new dream
foliage to cloth and
extend my essence,
to make me
majestic again.

Sleepy Fog

A California Zephyr train
passed over a river
named Platte at dawn,
traveling from
Denver to Chicago.
A scarlet sky met
white fog lain earth with a
light morning kiss and a
quiet embrace.
My mind sketched it,
but words couldn't memory
paint its mystical beauty.
Fog caressed earth with a
near weightless blanket over
hills, grass and trees.
It captured my soul with
unforgettable beauty, yet
I struggled to realize
its day to day created
time well spent beauty.
Fog soon evaporated like
love given and taken away.
Sun's crimson ambiance
softly stretched as far as
my eye could see.
Between river and infinity
laid God's work,
brushed with a word,
painted with a smile and
confirmed by my
human awareness.

Sleep Well

Yesterday four shirts and
two pairs of pants,
were enough to give
security and confidence.
One pair of shoes
protected feet well enough.
One coat and hat
provided a place to be
warm forever it seemed.

I now solicit more as
simplicity fades while
inequality spins
towards contempt.
Shiny success elevates
confidence as
glow of jewelry and a
silver walking stick
beat back intruders.

Much is too little and
little is left behind.
Where are those simple
gloves and socks needed?
Where is modesty that
made sleep so effortless?
I fear a cold grave
soon awaits me while
wearing one black suit.

Or Do I?

I sit quietly,
falling leaf listening,
red, yellow and
gold floats on air
like lost memories.
Leaves forget
their beginning,
earth returning
with no remorse.

Seeds are tree
parts that
can live again,
become again, but
leaves have no
memory and fall
reluctantly in
ignorance and
without promise.

Earth parts are
confusing because
some are seeds and
some are leaves,
some live long and
some die soon, but
in my listening
I learn much
about life.

No One Is to Blame

Blame settles
Not in one heart,
But spreads its
Wings and
Flies like a
Casting shadow
Over tear
Soaked faces
Exposed to
Guilt.

I say
Fly not
Dark faithful
Blame for
You shall
Not live or
Seek refuge
In any
Sensitive heart
Anymore.

An eagle's
Grace
You have not,
But only a
Buzzard's hunger,
So be gone
Blame's casting
Shadow for
All here are
Innocent.

Nature Belongs

In a wide
green valley of a tree
lined river enclave,
Nature resonates.

I feel cheek caress,
hair brush and
allow my soul to
gather memories.

Muddy water rushes
past my canoe,
paddle churns an
oblique course.

I hear Her speak,
teach and comfort as
I gently allow
essence meld.

Two eagles soar,
one skims water to
catch an
unaware fish.

Glory besets me,
humanity is
fortunate for
Nature touches.

Philosopher

My mouth is large and
teeth are yellow.
Can you hear
my breath?
It says go away.
I'm never in
direct middle of
anything important.
I tend to be a
little extreme.
I drink some wine,
sip it too well
some say, and
when I'm ready to
expound, don't
stand too close.

I have a friend
who speaks widely
like me and
his curly hair
hangs so low
you can't see
his eyes.
We go on and
on at lunch and
into bookish night.
He thinks this and
I think that,
philosophy seeks
no perfection
beyond us.
We know it all by

asking each other
opinions.
We like correct
answers and
recognize them
when delivered by
each other.

My fertile zest
lost its seed
long ago.
I gain little
traction or
seep no new
philosophy.
My numb mind,
that thing
I nearly lost a
few years ago,
now sits in solid
perfection of
lost distinction.

How Different Am I?

Don't come
down here,
climb trees,
eat foliage or
sit on a
warm stone.
Don't feel
rain and
sunlight that
teases earth.

I once
thought this
place was
paradise,
but life does
teach unfairness
even to a small
green frog
living in a
patio pot.

I am no
different than
others living in
confining spaces,
fearing change.
Time is often
criminal and needs
forgiveness for
its inevitable
death summons.

I'm not odd
living in a
fragile habitat,
fearing some
unnatural force
will reach
down and carry
me away with
some evil
hand.

Ok, I hide
pretending it is
forever safe,
fooling myself
while waiting a
rainy sky, a
freezing
cold day or a
consuming
hot sun.

It is, however,
peaceful now,
but don't come
down here.
Let me dream of
climbing trees,
eating foliage and
sitting on a
warm stone
by myself.

Fat Geese

Fat contented
river geese
symmetrically
swim in
structured
fashion,
squawking
goose words as
midday sun
glitters off
water crests.
Several
groupies
swim behind
one intrepid
leader
practicing
liberation.
Security and
freedom
intermingle as a
natural
approach to
good behavior
encourages
bravery.

I Used to Fear Night

I used to
pull a blanket
over my head
so to not hear
night sounds
speaking and
see demons
threatening.
I feared night
inside my head
you see,
too much
scary stuff
going on
in there.
I missed
night's
real wonder.

Now older,
with fear in
pocket and
night in hand,
I now
mind gaze and
wish to touch,
smell and
taste night.
I'm beginning
to understand
why poets
get inspired
by night.

On back
I lay until
summer's
night emerges,
stars filling
eyes, then
dreams teasing
mind.
It is as if
I am a
student cook
broiling and
baking
night notions
until dawn.

I am always
mentally
hungry yet
remain lean.
Night feeds
dreams and
dreams
tell secrets,
taking me a
billion
light years
from home.
I am now a
dream chef
who has
earned a
PhD in
"Night Studies."

Mental Sojourn

Dare I delve
into mind for
primordial and
deviant matter?
Dare I seek
abnormal and
peculiar history,
like coal or
oil deposits
beneath
mental surface?

Everything
waits discovery,
like a volcano
seeking release
of accumulated
pressure.
Dare I drill,
dig or
excavate for
answers and
knowledge?
In mind,
I fear a
buried place of
devil dancing and
angel singing.
I faintly feel
courage seeping
expression like
magma teasing a
mountain.

I gaze
within as if
mind is a
deep volcano.
I vividly see
conviction
creating
black sand.
I amusingly
delve further
into complex
mind that
makes me at
same time
weep and
laugh.

Yes, I dare
drill, dig and
excavate for
answers and
knowledge.
Yes, I dare
spill guts, and
leak inner
passions and
primordial
buried matter.
With fear and
courage
I mentally sojourn,
transforming
magma thoughts
into black
wisdom sand.

My Dreams

Dreams
flow easily as
fantasy ignores
reality during
idle night, but
seeks bits and
pieces in
morning light as
far as a mind
can see.

I learn
mind lessons
taught by
sketchers and
movie makers
calling-up
dreams.
I see past and
future in
odd places
where anything
is possible.

I wish to
stay in this
mental state
awhile,
reaping
passion while
provoking
life predictions.

I morning
remember
dream parts of
bedtime's
wondrous
adventure.
Only remnants
remain like
high tide
ocean debris.

Faint lessons
linger, but
I am not
changed or
more astute.
I cannot
appreciate
remnants and
suspect that
dreams are
empty night
blemishes.
Maybe life
itself is
only debris
collecting and
illusion
forgetting.

Truth

At times
I'm fuzzy,
juicy and
tasty like a
peach where
mind is
my pit.

I'm
seldom held,
bitten or
made to reveal
myself, but
I fear time is
my enemy.

I'll perish
someday and
only my pit
will remain to
liberate and
germinate
wisdom.

Chapter XI

Transitions

When we first took our small seventeen and a half foot boat out on the Carrabelle River, we had no idea what the red and green signs placed in the river water meant. I soon learned that there are buoys and day markers of red and green colors with numbers painted on them.

Buoys are attached to the bottom of the river and float while day markers are attach to post placed in the riverbed. The numbers indicate mileage up river. Buoys and day markers indicate where the channel is located and where one can navigate safely.

Spring of 2012

I steer our little white boat up river against a slow current, heading towards a place called "the glory hole," for possible fishing. Red day markers on starboard and green on port side guide me through the river channel. "Red right return," I think to myself as I remember the seaman's rule for traveling upstream and returning home from the sea.

I gaze northward, up river seeing Deborah sitting ahead of me, watching water, grass and trees create a moving picture like a mental movie, for in this sort of time we find many simple life aspects to cherish and remember.

I yet vividly recall when I met Debi, I had most everything needed while living in the country, in my little white house, and cherishing freedom and the lack of responsibility. I had much to lose and little to gain it seemed, and like most activities in life, I was getting more than I gave.

I, however, lost several things when I met Deborah. I lost loneliness, boredom and selfishness. She has given me much love, attention and respect. I didn't know I was lonely until I found true companionship. I didn't know I was bored until I gained her silent presence. I didn't know I was selfish until I began giving her little natural things from my heart.

Therefore, as we travel up-river in a little white boat, eager to catch fish and quietly sit in the sun, we do not really care if we get there or not, find the glory hole or catch that big fish for dinner.

I steer through red and green day makers until they end and we are in free finding channel with no further guidance, much as we are in life as guideposts, day markers and most enlightening signs are behind us. At our older age, there are few day markers other than our conscience and the Holy Spirit, but in the remaining guiding aspects we struggle some, yet have confidence that we are on the correct path, traveling the correct highway and steering up the correct river channel.

In our meeting six years ago, we found quiet humanitarian revelry with few expectations. We both wished our lives to be simple and easy. We wished no power or control, no psychological games or jealous adventures. We only wished to exercise our natural introverted personality and our desire for privacy.

In our life long struggle to be free, me being successful and Debi finding difficulty, freedom finally came to us willingly. We are still growing like flowers in a garden of security, with rain, sun and soul feeding our stem, branches and leaves. Buds appear and blossoms gather with our life awareness.

Little attention do we need from others for in our own garden we plant and harvest much by which to live and multiply. Our seeds are nearly useless now, but our ever-refined plant is yet healthy. Our pollen seeds fly no more in wind with prospect of another child, but our germination continues on with children and grandchildren.

It matters not that we have grand plans or seek high social position for we have served an earthly purpose so far and now seek only a higher purpose, for heaven speaks our name and we hear God whisper. He brought us together in the first place. We agree He was involved and now we try to show thanksgiving for His intervention.

"Red right return," I whisper as I recall the last red day marker, realizing I will have to think oppositely when going back down the river. I will have red on my left and green on my right side.

I think figuratively about going down stream in life, mooring our little white boat to a dock and maybe never taking it out again. Every day is like going up stream for the last time and I enjoy it more and more each blessed day. No one knows how many days they have left to live.

Debi and I certainly don't know our remaining days in life together, but then we think in years not days anyway. Few people ever know how many upriver cruises remain in their lives and if they do know, it is surely not because of enjoyable knowledge. The river itself has been here millions of years. Why couldn't Debi and I have at least twenty more years together? Maybe someday we will have to buy a new boat because we have out lived this one or maybe this is the last boat we will ever own. Oh, "red right return," keep showing me the way home.

Precious Stone

I found a
small stone,
cool narrow
stream resting,
another
considered it
useful, but
I valued it
precious.

It was not a
diamond,
ruby or even an
emerald, but a
creek rock
just like me,
shiny and
smooth
from years
of abiding
water and
abrasive silt.

Little did
I know a
silent
creek rock
could whisper
caring
words and
touch with
gentle
attention.

And when
calendars and
clocks point to
time's
fast passing,
I shall
remember a
higher power
brought
us together
in same
cool creek,
same deep,
slow moving
water flow.

My natural
awareness
sought
mind,
spirit and
soul while
learned
acceptance
engaged
past,
present and
future as
love
coalesced
opportunity.

Flower Basket

In naive basket
I gather years,
some beautiful,
some ordinary
some haunting.
Recollections
glorify and
demonize details.

My memory is a
melancholy
voice imparting
muted words.
I know
history, but
wrestle with
present reality.

Over mental
forearm
I carry this
enduring basket,
heavier and
heavier
it becomes
to my delight.

My basket is
my soul,
created with
intricate spiritual
substance and
formed from

God's own
existence.

God only
knows such
basket making.
Only He
can teach
earthly flower
gathering that
glorifies.

I finally
realize that
my basket,
full of all
experiences,
observes and
exemplifies
my life.

Tranquil Living

Just yesterday
I was easily
Carrabelle River
boating at six
miles per hour,
thinking while
observing with
self-disciplined
intelligence.

I considered
myself very
blessed for
having lived
long enough to
philosophize
myself into
being quiet and
tranquil.

But, reasoning
said change
was vital and
giving little
while gaining
much was
self-centered,
introverted
and anti-social.

Seems
my last night
dream was a

nightmare, a
constructive
nightmare,
critically
teaching a
lesson.

My dream
taught that
less is more,
then is good,
now is better, but
future is dear and
something to
courageously
penetrate.

There's a
thin line
between
dream and
nightmare,
fantasy and
reality,
more and
less.

I decided to
remain blessed,
letting mind
flow like an
uncontrolled
river while
allowing soul to
tranquilly
flourish.

Our Song

She hummed a
memorable
melody.
My heart
sang a
tomorrow
song, but
our brief
encounter
could not
grasp or
stand time
still.
It was like
trying to stop a
melting glacier.
Our short
lived world was
inevitably only
shared moments.
Our song of
relinquished
tears and
days together
was only a
lost illusion
in an old
scrapbook.

Living Art

They thought
only glass or
pottery
resembled
fragility and
capable of
shattering.

They didn't
remember
training,
military,
war or
living life
tough.

They didn't
remember
sports,
marriages,
children or
teaching
forty years.

They forgot
traveling
carries own
risks while
night moving
towards a
far enemy.

They never
observed
falling short
when
experiencing
risky slopes
alone.

They didn't
hear
requests for
help or
witness
collapse of
altered mind.

Apt courage
transforms
ugliness into
dignity when
freedom and
living art
remain.

A mislaid
glass or
pottery piece
yet possesses
resilience and an
aware man can
identify it.

Youthful Courage

On a
dream edge
I stood,
fearful to
step as if a
dark abyss
wished to
swallow what
little daring
remained.

I discovered,
however,
no leap was
necessary,
only crawling,
then stepping as
I foolishly
dragged my
cowardly
body.

From fantasy
to reality,
to insight
I stabilized
myself,
reasoning that
even one step
can sometimes
be executed
courage.

Soil of My Soul

Soil of my
persistent soul
grows flowers that
few understand or
care to discover.

I share a
short time with
each seed,
like a sea wave
in ocean's mirth.

My gardens,
beaches and
mountains are
where
I began and
where
I will end.

Inches Apart

We sit apart
saying nothing,
gazing through a
windshield while
asphalt yields and
countryside passes.
We gather
thoughts
while sunlight
squinting and
hypnotic engine
listening.
We simultaneously
pull down
sun visor and
stay speechless
in comfortable
silence.
Trite chatter is
needless when
knowing a
private soul
needs little
adoration.
Mutual
appreciation
speaks with
gestures,
glances and
touches at an
amazing
volume.

Sure Hand

She traced a
sure hand
down jaw bone
towards mouth,
lightly and
gently as
shared
mature beauty.
Sunburned,
unshaven skin
caused touch to
seem fake,
but with
graceful hand
she further
explored
mouth and
expressed
valid love.
She clasp
face and
held body,
mind and
soul essence,
showing
affection and
igniting
passion.

Important Aspects

Life now is
short on
important
aspects, yet
long on
trivial
aspects.
I avoid
things that
make me
hurt and
call out for
help,
things that
give me
fear and
needed
redemption.

Oh, I can
count and
dismiss, but
I cannot
forget, for
within lies
my history
waiting to
recall itself.

I gladly
seek memory
loss and
forgetfulness

gain.
There are few
important
aspects to
life now.
Remaining
aspects
concern
others outside
myself and
my future
somewhat
belongs to
children and
grandchildren.

My unknown
new years wait
somewhere in
time and space
while old years
get measured by
my stories and
poems.

Time is yet
ambiguous and
similar to when
I was young.
It changes and
makes most
everything a bit
uncomfortable.

Life now feels
melancholy,

like a familiar
odd mixture of
old faith and
new hope.
I yet live life,
like when a
young man
tasting red wine.
It yet makes
me a little bit
drunk.

Remnants

Wilted flowers
in a humble
vase share
sorrow and
regret with
forlorn songs
lamenting
lost life and
gained heaven.

Soon flower
remnants
get scattered
on a field,
organic
again and
spiritually
aware of
silent passing.

Holy and
soulful
containers
also become
organic as
time devours
everything with a
taste for
evolution.

This Old House

I pause to
see and hear
tree leaves
dancing while
facing wind with
watering eyes.
Leaf death
seems long ago.
Spring now
comes to
remind with
glorious
rebirth and
eternal renewal.

One tree allows
ten thousand
green leaves to
murmur and
together they
create a loud
musical drone.
Then ten more
lush trees
together
play a
graceful
thriving wind
symphony.

I sway to a
moody melody,
slowly dancing
my way home.

I close eyes,
open mind and
gather peace
within my
grasping soul.
I pray that
I shall enter
heaven with
just such a
disposition.

o

Howling and
whining wind
passes through a
splintered
old house,
causing
enchanting
music to
tease my
open mind.

Images of
bent siding and
distorted shutters
seemingly wink and
grin at me.
Time has taken
its toll and
yet pride displays
its own
resilient reward.

A mother held
her infant here.

Security and
peace was
learned here.
Now a soothing
wind melody
murmurs in
tree and
house remnants.

o

Gone are
those who
made this
place survive.
No one will
return here
except to
trash and
carry away
what is left.

Feeble
electrical wiring,
bent propane
gas pipe,
buckled
flooring and
curled linoleum
have surely
failed time's
harsh test.

Unsightly
wallpaper
hangs from
forbearing walls.

Light fixtures
that will never
electrically
glow again
lifelessly
ceiling sway.

Youth met
maturity here,
maturity met
death here and
time stole
nearly everything
except precious
memories waiting an
old man's
recollection.

Running With Snow

Moon reflects
light off
snow covered
pasture paths where
horses wandered
during afternoon.
But now cold
driving snowflakes
assemble as a
blizzard chariot
ready to be attached
to harness.
It mentally invites
me through
time and space.

I knowingly
fantasy fly as
might a unique
snow storm
bide time,
knowing its
short existence
will soon end.
This mental
night blizzard
is bits and
pieces of
my life
passing as
snow drifts
mound and
form memories.

Ice horses are
then attached to
my chariot and
gallop like
emancipated
frozen emissaries.
I rein guide
them with mind
while reflecting
my life history.
Snow threatens to
lower me
into an ominous
ice casket.
I pull scarf
over my
spoiled mind and
hurl unruly
thoughts at
cold harsh life.

I then race
from night and
into morning sun as
snow subsides and
time apologizes.
My mind powered
snow chariot halts.
Dreaming teases a
white pastured
mind no more.
Gathered snow
melts into time and
space beyond where
I night traveled
beyond reality.

I gaze out
through a frost
covered window,
seeing no
blizzard remnants.
Only a mind
yet seeking
illumination remains.

I sit for
several minutes
thinking and
remembering,
reasoning that
dreams are
subconscious
messages from a
fascinating
mind place.
I ponder wisdom
gained and
find little
correlation to
real life.
I reason that
dreams might
construct
philosophy,
viewpoints and
possibilities, but an
awake mind
associates and
correlates facts to
predict future
solutions.

Holy Blanket

We use our
threads and
needles to
place life's
fabric seams,
dressing
our souls and
wrapping
our spirits
in a woven
holy blanket.

Conclusion

Everything is a dichotomy with a beginning and an ending, and our nearly unaware existence operates amidst an infinite number of bipolar extremes.

We cannot escape seeking and finding compromise in most aspects of our lives; and yet there are life areas beyond negotiation. These aspects are called principles, and principles should be limited to a few because we might have to go to war over them.

Morality and ethics predicate principles based on honesty, integrity and honor. The finding of middle ground between two extremes can get complicated. Therefore, I suggest the need for simplicity into the mix of middle ground questing.

We are like a sailing ship at sea on a calm day when sunlight is seeking our joy and blue water is washing our minds pure. Then a storm approaches from the West, high winds threaten, and from out of nowhere a great white squall hits. All we can then say as Jeff Bridges shouts in the movie, White Squall, "We're in it now," and then endeavor to remain alive.

So I conclude that one must find simple ways to live within extremes through awareness of life, and when extremes do appear, we spiritually conduct ourselves the best we can while maintaining balance, keeping our ship afloat until death transforms us correctly. I think for me personally being steered by the Holy Spirit is the answer to dichotomy middle sailing.

The second greatest dichotomy is life and death,

but the first greatest is heaven and hell, thus for a Christian, saving one's soul depends on a single extreme choice, believing in Jesus. All other extremes are middle ground tolerable.

I suspect there are no dichotomies in heaven. Oh, what a wonderful time it will be to get a temporary reprieve from dichotomies. I fear I will keep returning to Earth until I get it right, returning to find purity and learn true spirituality. I seek wisdom like the Lord's prayer says, "on Earth as it is in Heaven." My old soul yet struggles to gain wisdom as my ever-young spirit seeks only its home.

I wish strength
and guidance to
` live another day as
extremes probe
mind and body, and
dichotomies seek
my soul's divide.

About Author

Phillip Reisner is a product of Midwestern values; he, however, pushes, pulls and adjusts these values to fit a slightly different life philosophy. He judiciously finds middle ground to many life situations. He grew up on an Indiana farm, yet even today he finds opportunities to experience life far beyond the farm.

He worked at a bank, served in the military, earned BS and MS degrees, and taught school for thirty years. Phillip is now retired yet finds time to swim, volunteer, travel and write. He is married to Deborah, and they collectively have six children and eleven grandchildren.

Phillip writes short stories in prose and poetry. Every concise narrative provokes thinking. His poems use minimal words with each short line standing alone and making a point. Every word is meaningful and important and that is just how he feels about every day and every person, meaningful and important.